MW00425743

Night

2,000 Haiku
By man and machine

D. H. Cope

Some of the following haiku were written by my computer programs and some by great Japanese haiku poets such as Kobayshi Issa, Matsuo Basho, and Yosa Buson (translated into English). Both categories include multiples of hundreds in number. Can you tell which is which? Do only some have meaning? Are some worthwhile? Does the large number of poems presented here make the one seem less important?

Most of the poems have seventeen syllables in the form 5-7-5. The ones that don't are caused by difficulties in translation or by allowing the computer program to make mistakes. If you're looking for giveaways, remember that haiku can be humorous as well as pithy, happy, prophetic, sad, and historical.

Don't let the number 2,000 fool you. Issa wrote many hundreds of haiku. So guessing machine-created by number alone will not make it so.

Please forgive obvious mistakes as they appear. I've kept punctuation to a minimum here since the computer output does not have it. Note that translations from the Japanese are anonymous and any resemblance to other translations is strictly coincidental.

If you feel you have made correct choices as to which haiku were created by humans and which by machine, you can mail your choices to me at howell@ucsc.edu and I'd be happy to give you your score. But I won't tell you which is which for fear you might make it known and ruin it for others.

Note that if you read one of these a day (better than reading them all in one sitting), you won't finish for well over five years.

You may reprint one or more of these haiku freely with the provision that you acknowledge the source and the copyright exactly.

All proceeds from the sale of this book will go to Greenpeace, the largest independent direct-action environmental agency in the world.

David Cope 2011

1

Comes the fiery night,
When all those gone return,
None the brighter for it.

2

Inevitable
Beauties of the daring seas
Do tasteless egos write.

3

With guilty conscience,
I step out the door of my hut
And find her waiting.

4

Leaving on a trip,
My drought stricken trees
Give me somber memories.

5

Shadows in the
Drifting snows of winter's
Night were interrupted.

6

When the thunder sleeps,
Where glacial meadows follow,
Then tall the snow falls.

7

Too few fat catfish
Linger along the shores here
For the fishermen.

8

A long hard journey,
Rain beating down the clover
Like the wanderer's feet.

9

Slipping silently,
A sand turtle toddles his
Way home for the night.

10

Grandfather told me
That nothing would be easy.
Too hard in that case.

11

Searching for a way,
The angry crow cries loudly
For its lost mother.

12

Standing in my way,
A robin steels the path from me
And hikes to its nest.

13

I caught a sea bass
A long way from home, on its
Journey to spawn.

14

When I pause to rest,
A large black growling bear
Finds solace in my fears.

15

Raising up my head,
A treasure appears above
In the form of stars.

16

A trail turns away
And gives me another choice
Of which way to go.

17

From this year on in
My left hand, my umbrella
Hates my right knapsack.

18

Birds-nest soup agrees
With everyone but the birds
Who need it for eggs.

19

Honking ducks fly by
Making their presence known to
All of us who care.

20

The reeds bend to ground,
Hearing the rumble of geese
As they cross the stream.

21

No is an answer
No one wants to ever hear
Sitting next to a pond.

22
Through persimmon days,
Promote your eagernesses
In terms of robins.

23
How sad it would be
If the wren never got sad,
For sadness is proud.

24
At a roadside shrine,
Before the stone Buddha,
A firefly burns bright.

25
From far off I heard
The sounds of a whippoorwill
Singing in silence.

26
Isolation never
Hurts those who follow its way.
Or so says the bear.

27
The peaks that give peace,
Stand alone along the trail
Giving me quiet times.

28
A valley stream goes
Quietly by my hut and
Gives me pleasure.

29
Crows have few cronies,
Living as they do in groups
That never give up.

30
Birds on a sill chirping
Ever so loudly in tune
On a windy day.

31
Along came a mouse,
Waiting for me to feed it,
But not as a mouse.

32
In the spring, sea waves
Undulating and undulating
All the day long.

33
The glacier waterfalls
Melt off the mountain into my
Very dry garden.

34
With cherry blossoms gone,
A temple is seen
Through twigs and branches.

35
Several herons
Followed along with my small
Younger godchildren.

36
At sunset, the sound
Of guns shooting pheasants near
Spring mountainsides.

37
A ghost turned sideways,
Expecting me to not see
That it could not see me.

38
The river winds blow,
Giving the surface no plan
Of how to proceed.

39
Butterfly in my hand,
As if it were a spirit,
Unearthly, insubstantial.

40
Joys come very slow,
While sadness lasts forever
In the vast outdoors.

41
The craftsman's straw cape,
Brocaded with the storm-strewn
Cherry blossoms.

42
Waiting for a black cat
Never gives me much pleasure,
For late is normal.

43
The calligraphers
Rid themselves of thoughts of
Tender miracles.

44
Spring's setting sun
Treads on the train of a
Mountain-crest pheasant.

45
Rainbows assembled
Their minions for all the sweet
Forever afters.

46
My hut leans forward
Toward the end of the island
Where it and I sit.

47
Wooden crutches stand
Where I cannot, and give me
Strength where I cannot.

48
Why cannot I be
As happy as a robin,
And not as a crow?

49
Amidst the grassland
Sings a skylark, free and
Unlimited from all things.

50

Cavernous ruins
Call to me from their hideouts
Where I can't find them.

51

A single raindrop
Makes its mark in the sandy
Ground beneath my feet.

52

In the cicadas cry,
No sign can foretell
How soon it will die.

53

The shadows of clouds
Amble along behind me,
Pushing me forward.

54

Clouds appear
And bring men a chance to rest
From looking at the moon.

55

In light from the moon,
The raven standing alone
Calls for its lover.

56

Harvest moon,
Around the pond I wander,
Throughout the night.

57
Along the river,
An inchworm wiggles its way
Towards the deep water.

58
From the chill of night,
Waiting for the cold before
Dawn's earliest light.

59
How many robins
Can find their way in the dark
Just as worms do?

60
High in the night sky,
I hear the faraway voice
Of my grandfather.

61
Limbs bend to the ground
Under weight of old snow
Bound for the river.

62
Too many mockingbirds
Make telling their stories hard
If anyone listens.

63
A grave near my house
Stood for many years quietly
Waiting for me.

64
In the silence proud,
Came the harshest winds of time,
Setting me backward.

65
Chasing the rainbow
Gives robins their exercise,
And many other things.

66
The moon glows at night.
What does it take for that to
Change us forever?

67
Several blackbirds
Gathered in a field afar,
And told us to leave.

68
Gentle touch repels
Its happiness, while ever
Hiding its lost poor.

69
The shores of Japan
Gave us his first taste of love,
The bear told us.

70
A gentle breeze blew,
Not tipping me over nor
Standing me upright.

71

The bottomless pail
Waits for the berries to fall.
Hear them plunk their heads!

72

Golden mountain clouds
Bend the light reflected off
The desert's flowers.

73

Green smoke-covered reeds,
Flat arms caught grandfather's
Lucky robin gone ground.

74

Lucky grandmother
Suffered a yellow loon, ducked
In a star's hidden snow.

75

The widow's keepsake
Left us all in a lurch, for
Never would we know.

76

White snow in fall,
Brown snow in winter's deep,
Black snow in springtime.

77

The impossible man
Climbed the mountain where he
Gazed at immense fields of stars.

78

Too many blossoms
Leaves many a wasted plum
Lying on the ground.

79

Mount Fuji gives its
Best imitation of a
Great red warrior.

80

Dark moon tasted fire,
Caught the wind's lantern, grew
An egret as lasting child.

81

An early lesson
Produced no new medicine
For stupidity.

82

Gather all your gifts
In one place, and give thanks, for
There is nothing else.

83

Mountain caves provide
Shelter for the many that
Have no other home.

84

My mysterious
Isolated convictions
Posed aggressive thoughts.

85
Night is the only
Time in the world when all give
Thanks for the daytime.

86
Rain falls on the grass,
Filling the ruts left by
A carnival's wagon.

87
An evening cloudburst.
Sparrows cling desperately
To trembling branches.

88
Prancing meadowlarks
Decimated the meadow's land,
Making sand seem light.

89
My seeds have rough skins,
Giving them an extra chance
To grow against odds.

90
Tall clouds reach up to
Graze the shadow of the moon
And capture my heart.

91
My roof slants eastward
Toward the islands that tower
Over the sea and me.

92
A plough carves the plain
Into thousands of furrows
Deep in the mud boughs.

93
The rice fields watered
The mountains carrying rain.
My hut's dancing lights.

94
Castles in the mud
Cannot give hospice to crabs
Who never cared much.

95
The canyon keep
Provides a hollow place for
Me to spend my time.

96
Some frogs sound their horns.
Others keep the peace instead,
Never yet be gone.

97
Temple bells die out,
But fragrant blossoms remain.
A perfect evening.

98
A giant firefly
Moves this way and that
As it passes by.

99
Just one man.
Also a fly, just one.
In a huge drawing room.

100
I kill an ant,
But realize my three children
Have been watching.

101
A goat bleats at night,
A frog honks during the day,
And I stand alone.

102
Several eagles
Fly separately over
Land and sea homeward.

103
The wetlands follow
The tide pools around the beach,
Moving toward cliffs.

104
Tumbling over sand,
A large mouse finds itself tired,
And a scorpion, too.

105
A rice bowl tumbles
Over on its side into
A bucket of wine.

106
A long white egret,
A bright moonlit night above,
And nowhere to go.

107
Bluebirds sing at dawn.
Owls hoot in the night only.
Mockingbirds just sing.

108
The moment two bubbles
Are united, they both vanish,
And a lotus blooms.

109
Far too many times
My windows shook in the wind
Giving me shivers.

110
The waves on water
Roll in from their home ashore,
Leaving me standing.

111
Come the summertime,
My visions of nevermore
Gave me little love.

112
Several times a day,
The grandfather sought his son,
But never found him.

113
The acrid smoke grew,
As no one took the credit
For the fire that kills.

114
Eagles fly alone,
Never to fight the west winds,
Always going home.

115
Up against the wall,
A rake leans as if nothing
At all is amiss.

116
Birds at rest only
Seem at rest, but really not,
For they are alive.

117
Sleep comes not easy
To one who soars in the sky
And dives for cover.

118
Holding in my arms,
A misbegotten frog that
Needs a new mother.

119
Silence becomes me.
It settles like a blossom
Over the night air.

120

Wet the night becomes.
Flowers explode with color
And no one to see.

121

Summer erupted
Into thunderous flowing
Waterfalls near by.

122

Not too many men
Stand eye to eye with the bear,
But the rose gives way.

123

Puppets dancing here,
Clowns and acrobats in fear
That soon night will fall.

124

Moonlight in darkness.
What a shadow it casts
Over me and you.

125

The dark mountain pass
Reveals its terrors to the
Lost days that lie low.

126

Flying across skies,
A falcon looks down upon
Me and my kitten.

127
All of a sudden,
Six blackbirds appear to me,
Standing in a line.

128
How can I forget
That summer has gone away
And winter has come?

129
Obedient forms
And beautiful roses have
Sticky heads and necks.

130
Remember those days
When sorrow was forever?
And now is gone.

131
Her demonstration
Meant that her lovely lips
Gave sweet temptations.

132
Wandering around,
I found a now dead clover
Reaching out to me.

133
What can I do now
That the sun has gone downward
Into the dark water?

134
Tell me the story
Where the one I love loves me
But I do not care.

135
Have you no pity
For the meadowlark that weeps?
Have you no sorrow?

136
Rain creeps in my hut,
And leaves me with no dry rice
For my meal tonight.

137
Daughters and sons laugh,
Catching the wind in their souls
And letting it go.

138
Falling down today,
I heard a crow make its call,
Laughing as it did.

139
Too many crows flying
For no good reason today.
Why not tomorrow?

140
On New Years Day,
I longed to meet my parents
As they were before my birth.

141

The crow has flown away.
Swaying in the evening sun,
A leafless tree.

142

Rice field maidens stand.
The only things not muddy
Are the songs they sing.

143

The pushcart pushes,
And the old man pulls backwards,
And no one will win.

144

Wind socks blow fiercely,
Giving directions for none.
Why were they put there?

145

Next to the morning's
Meal, a meadowlark seeks out
The friendship of me.

146

Buddha asks me how
I can wander aimlessly,
With so much to do.

147

Moments of glory
Waste their time with me today,
For I know not why.

148
A sorrowful wren
Looks out upon the meadow
And wonders aloud.

149
Falcons don't attack,
But rather fall on their prey
As they devour them.

150
Few hens lay their eggs
In the yard by my warm hut
Without crowing first.

151
Following the wind,
The flower petals rise high
And leap to their death.

152
Silly little bees,
Woken by strange echoes of
Tomorrow's fireflies.

153
Never finding fate
Gives me the idea that
Fate will still find me.

154
The cliffs of wonder
Make risks the more enduring.
Or so says the bear.

155
Snakes lift their bodies
Out of the water into
The nests of bluebirds.

156
Fantastical
Sounds in the dead of night give
Those who hear them dread.

157
Children playing in
Sand on the beach gives one pause,
And makes me think.

158
Fog covers my flowers,
Hiding their beauty in the
Belly of its soul.

159
The high mountain peaks
Glow in the night's darkness
Above me tonight.

160
After killing
A spider, how lonely I feel
In the cold of night.

161
Seventeen children
Have never seen so much snow
That they cannot dream.

162

A rainstorm coming
To the castle village king
And the sergeant's arms.

163

Fish sleep in water
Under the bridges I cross
When I follow you.

164

Sitting under a tree,
In the shade of its high limbs,
Its leaves sticking to me.

165

Hollowed out dry logs
Give ants and groundhogs places
For bears to find them.

166

The dark shadows move,
Catching flies in their cradles
And blowing bubbles.

167

How did my mother
Know what to do when I cried?
And does anyone?

168

The great waterfall
Greets me after all today.
When I least thought so.

169
My eternal youth
Provided just three cents of
The emperor's pine.

170
Where icicles fall,
No one may wander again
Except for the snow.

171
Green castles provide
My life with so much wonder
That the bear gave up.

172
For love and hate,
I swat a fly and offer it
To an ant.

173
The summer river flows,
And though there is a bridge, my
Horse goes through the water.

174
Hearing the ground growl
Gives one a better knowledge
Of what is coming.

175
The winds that blow
Asks them which leaf on a tree
Will be next to go.

176

Shadows penetrate
Our souls because we cannot
Find ourselves in them.

177

A gold bug
Hurls itself into darkness
And feels the depth of night.

178

Crying as if life
Can never give up one's thoughts,
Nor bring death along.

179

Singing a sad song
Can make all things seem lonely.
A raven calls out!

180

Tall pines smell like dusk
Of a long winter's moonlight.
Desolate and dead.

181

Nothing I can do
Will make the dew brighter or
Wetter than it is.

182

Pink flowers grow slow
As the days pass us glowing
For their precious lives.

183

Cannot they see now
How the fisherman fishes,
And the heron hunts?

184

Never mind the snow.
It whitens as you go,
Without an end in sight.

185

A black bear hunts fish
In lakes by the sea, wherein
Lie the shores of life.

186

Sleeping during days
Causes my memory to
Wander all over.

187

One kills the other.
Not so nice it seems to me,
Cats and mice do play.

188

How can my heart beat
When so many nights have passed
With nothing to show?

189

Far too many ducks
Fly above me into clouds,
Beating their wings hard.

190

The poet sings songs
And the night listens in fear
That nothing will grow.

191

Glorious nightmares
Follow me wherever I go,
Now that the winter's gone.

192

A chrysanthemum.
Growing crooked's a thing it
Knows nothing about.

193

Calling them homeward,
The children seem lonely, how
Can that truly be true?

194

The stronger the taste,
The more that the hunger wastes
Its energies on me.

195

I can hear the wrens
Rustling in the brush near me
Following their mates.

196

Several robins
Gathered together to sing
Of nothing at all.

197
The moon so bright it
Tells me of centuries of
A bright light at night.

198
Hummingbirds fluttering
Around a hibiscus plant,
Seem to never land.

199
A bear hugs a tree,
Shaking it back and forth and
Back again in haste.

200
The tops of tall trees.
The never-ending snowfall
Descending on us.

201
The tall grasses smell,
The mountains glow with
Moonlight, tonight the bear stalks.

202
The stream and the cat,
Irony and paradox,
Fighting for their lives.

203
Too many chances
For the tern to escape him,
So the bear gave up.

204
Standing on a chair,
Reaching for the moon tonight,
And not catching it.

205
Thistles block my way,
Thunder up above rumbles,
Impossible to stop.

206
The snails in my yard
Wander about with no thoughts
About what to eat.

207
Alternative life.
Wings flapping in every way.
Butterflies mating.

208
The golden windows
Reflect the sun's light about
My room as I watch.

209
Too many loons now
Calling out to each other,
With no one listening.

210
Around the road's bend
I can now see the future,
As if in wonder.

211
The mud around me
Gives no hope for escape
From the depths of life.

212
Snakes slither around,
Following the smells of the
Grasses around them.

213
The light of my fire
Glows in the darkness tonight
And gives me a chill.

214
Several shallow
Calligraphers promoted
The drab followers.

215
The wind blows softly.
The morning air does thus
Breathe, and life continues.

216
The shores of the lake
Give life to the herons that
Flock to the forest.

217
Her temptations
Frustrated his advances
Into careless dreams.

218

Few know the secret
That no one else can find here,
Because it's not.

219

Ice fields lay sprawling
Across the glacier's wide path.
Nothing tender here.

220

Dark shadows follow
Wherever I go tonight,
Thought the whippoorwill.

221

Butterflies touch ground
Rarely as they flit from here
To their destiny.

222

The lights in the sky
Make the darkness seem friendly
Whenever I wish.

223

Patterns in the light
Make me see clouds differently,
The bear sat thinking.

224

A cup of green tea
Makes you and me happier,
My friend and friend's friend.

225
The limbs of a tree
Bend toward the ground where
They lay down their fruits.

226
Kites flew blindly on,
As the hated windy storm's
Rainy thunderclouds.

227
Washing my window
Makes thinking easier than
Looking though the glass.

228
Animated pens,
Beautiful lakes, and gentle
Dark innocence.

229
In honor of sadness,
Only those who have not felt
Can participate.

230
The deep hell of souls
Glorified the painful gifts
Of heaven's gateways.

231
Your loud wind chimes
Gave yet their vocabulary,
Closed all books and poems.

232
Snow falling in the
Mountains, with the summer's
Heat. Floods coming today.

233
Breathing it all in,
A spider looks after its young
And not backward.

234
Small wisdoms impart
Seldom used advice giving
Nothing in advance.

235
How many muskrats
Standing on the fallen tree
Staring right at me?

236
A brief thunderstorm
Passes us by on our way
Home to the garden.

237
Black dragonflies pawed
Her babies, while their heaven
Boasts of ministers.

238
Too many gophers
Give me a headache today,
And tomorrow too.

239
What makes me so sad,
A broken heart or love
That cannot be found.

240
Your ancient numbers
Disqualify dragons and
Their information.

241
Confluent rivers
Stand together as one, now
That the floods have come.

242
Forget me nots do
What they are not named to do,
For I forgot them.

243
Stupidity flinched,
When your wisdom gave up its
Tormented hatred.

244
Walking home today,
I saw a bright flash above,
And wondered of you.

245
Happenstance can be
Ever so lonely a spot
For me to find you.

246
Catch a meadowlark
And listen to it sing songs,
Nevermore to be.

247
A simple kiss can,
After all else has been done,
Resurrect lovers.

248
Sacrificial lambs,
Bad experiences made
Petite novelettes.

249
His flatulent
Bones destroyed his awareness
Of her innocence.

250
Death stalks at a pace
Closing slowly on my own
Now that winter's here.

251
In the snow below me,
Indentations with here and there
The tracks of cougars.

252
Several students
Share their minds with each other,
Not minding at all.

253

Cartons of rice cakes
Sit by my door and wonder
What the bear would say.

254

Golden meadowlarks
Stand by the side of the path
And whistle at me.

255

Give me your hunger,
And I will feed it to my
Lover's mysteries.

256

Robins surrendered mountains, and
Meadows, and straight
The weak will now walk.

257

Never and ever,
Two words that do not matter
To me or others.

258

Fewer though they be,
None can be prouder than the
Sacrificial lambs.

259

Lesser mortals stand,
Not on crimson tides or death,
But they stand on me.

260

Why do I care so
For the flowers that show me
The way to love them?

261

Sitting by my fire,
The stars show me all of their
Wonder and glory.

262

Can I really see
What the moon shows me tonight?
Or am I lonely?

263

A secluded house,
Even for a palm-sized rice
Cake, a commotion.

264

Cemeteries blew
A flower through the downtown
Rapid railway trains.

265

Others might think I'm
At my spring calligraphy.
My little window.

266

The smoke from the fire
Caused the robins and wrens
No end of worry.

267

In hot summer nights,
Gnats have their perfect tributes
To human frailty.

268

Watching the water
Flow down the mountain rock falls,
The bear notices.

269

Never trust a gull
Tracing figures in the sand.
It finishes not.

270

The hedgehog under
My hut has feathers. It seems
I cannot find him.

271

Her brilliance
Fought all the predictably
Mean arguments.

272

In the fall of night,
A pledge soon looses its right
To follow the light.

273

Egrets balanced high
On treetops over meadows.
Waiting till high tide.

274
Against all manner
Of predators and raptors,
Stands the lonely knight.

275
Forever is long
As the moon's dark shadow lifts
My spirits to thee.

276
Red roses provide
Happiness for all to see
In my maiden's eyes.

277
The path swerves around
My hut and then moves into
The forest's dangers.

278
Those who know answers
Never seem to know the right
Questions that relate.

279
A knock on my door
Gives me a start and deepens
My fear of surprise.

280
My many-paged book
Mediated tradition
For all passengers.

281
Hawks fly high and far,
Giving all their fire to kill
Everything below them.

282
Wind chimes ring their bells
And wake the cockleshells for
Morning's wet embrace.

283
Secrets make life fun
For those who know the secrets.
Others not so much.

284
A sandpiper runs
Toward tomorrow as it pecks
Into the wet sand.

285
Find a deeper hole,
And in it put all that means
Something to your soul.

286
Grandfather never
Told those around him what he
Caught in the lake.

287
Haiku never fails
To confuse those who try and
Find its true meaning.

288
Embers in the wind,
The fireflies of the darkness,
Glowing in the night.

289
Too few red baskets
To fill with my blue flowers
While the thunder roars.

290
For festive jelly,
Use the venerable twelfth
Day of first winter rain.

291
His music smacked
Of their appreciation
And depredation.

292
His temperature
Sharpened so all their
Mental images straightened.

293
Flowers audited
Compulsory things, while round
My deep pedigrees.

294
Reeds sway back and forth
In the pond next to my house.
And the forest waits.

295
Fourteen blackbirds fly
Into the sky above me
And teach me to sing.

296
Tension whistled but
Surrendered all its men to
His crooked nightmares.

297
Bright the light off ice
When I encounter frozen
Lakes of winter.

298
When do the wild winds
Blow softly on my brow?
No one can answer.

299
When pirated mice
Untangled his migraines for
All of their ransoms.

300
Hidden from the view,
The thrush signals its mother
That everything's alright.

301
The dark hollow night
Chilled the sparrows to their
Death, sorrowing the day.

302
Your delivery
Eliminated tempers
Of short exhaustion.

303
Time penetrates all
With nothing left for others.
The bridge goes too far.

304
Never before now
Have the wildflowers grown high
In the night's darkness.

305
Aggravating flies.
Keep your distant skies away
From my guiltless skin.

306
Deadly catfish wait
Until the light is dim and
Dying for their meals.

307
Are you the nighttime
Bird's only daughter behind
The others singing?

308
The falcon flies high,
The meadowlark flies lower,
What's the difference?

309

Blackbirds in the night
Shine with the glow of the moon
On their flapping wings.

310

The wren's reflection
Gives off a luminescence
That lights the night sky.

311

The mangy wild dogs
Ran with the river and barked
Into the rain-swept night.

312

Several thousand
Worms stand in the warm
Meadow and stretch their sinews.

313

Wax flower eagles.
Wide icicles diagnosed.
Odd behaviors.

314

My back door opens.
Big red fox appears outside.
Clouds sail overhead.

315

Along a crocked road,
Appears a lone man walking
Toward the endless mote.

316
Too many robins
Crowd into the trees outside
And make life gentle.

317
My mysterious
Visitors leave me with
Abandoned kittens.

318
The territory
Printed with all your options.
How strong the minions.

319
Fall brings the dark rains
To wet the ground for winter.
The snow to follow.

320
Curved universes,
Curl back upon each other,
Until no one knows!

321
Dusk provides the hues
That keep us from going mad,
And the snake sleeps on.

322
Boats slide into slips
At night, as the fishing stops
And the sleeping starts.

323
Standing at the door
The old man looks upon the
Big black bear dancing.

324
When the rain falls, we
Hear it land around our hut
And wonder why so.

325
In all of my years,
Never have I wandered as
I have wandered now.

326
The chicken fox stares
Giving the hens a scary
Time to hide their chicks.

327
Twilight lends its edge
That cuts to the heart of all
Before they know it.

328
While reconciled, he
Abolished the dark typhoon,
But lost the battle.

329
Could you have chosen
Me without knowing my soul?
Never mind that now.

330
So few tears for me.
That must mean my balance with
Life is not in sight.

331
Tall the trees that stand
Upright in the winter's winds
Never bending low.

332
When we die alone
No one knows what keeps us from
Continuing on.

333
January slapped its
Rivers over white snowfields
Aware of daydreams.

334
Pine nuts give us joy,
Whatever tongues they might
Touch and teeth encounter.

335
Pine trees meet your death
When fire catches at your breath,
And gives you life again.

336
Seaweed salts your wounds.
Take your medicine to bed
And sleep until noon.

337
Birds fly up and down,
Sideways and around above
Where sky keeps them warm.

338
Shriek the mother hen
When vultures dive again to
Eat your youngest child.

339
My grandfather sleeps
Next to the old potbelly
Stove and snores loudly.

340
Pink and orange dawn,
So much joy to give to us all,
And no one watches.

341
The ruins of a town
Border the property I own
And never trespass

342
The rose fields scatter
Their seeds to the winds above
And we all prosper.

343
Could be a dozen
Fireflies coupling outside of
My hut here tonight.

344
Could it be that I
Have never really believed
In anything at all?

345
Sincereness had gone
The way of all the old things
Into the waste pile.

346
The cat chased the rat
Never forgiving it the
State of its affairs.

347
Two soft beds ready
For two soft bodies to lie
On their silky tops.

348
The greenish blue ducks
Flew southward toward the city
Leaving me behind.

349
Agonizing but
Ornate, he commandeered a
Pirate's ransom.

350
The reddish night skies
Gave the horizon a look
Of not belonging.

351
Clack goes another
Goose on his way to other
Places in the world,

352
Her icy anger
Countermanded orders from
All her attendants.

353
The edge of the lake
Ran up against the side of
My garden's roses.

354
Harbingers of truth
Rarely provide credentials
Of their equations.

355
Snails in their soft shells
Ponder the meaning of life.
And the Buddha sleeps.

356
Widow's weeping sons
Seldom ignore the kisses
Whenever given.

357
Birds fly everywhere,
Even in the darkest night,
While whippoorwills sleep.

358
The bright star I see,
Sees not me but another
Off in the distance.

359
Singing, planting rice.
Village songs more lovely
Than famous city ones.

360
A water spider
Suns on the lake's surface
Catching a short nap.

361
Standing at my gate,
A robin waits to enter
And gives it a push.

362
When identified,
Cherry trees give character
To a big black bear.

363
Shameless scoundrels lie
Under the trees where they watch
Me tending garden.

364
Corners of the sky
Stand as high as the crying
Of the nightingale.

365
What did the robin
Say to the blackbird today?
Never mind the rush!

366
Over the mountains
Several clouds begin to
Send their children forth.

367
Music playing soft
Over a great distance from my
House makes me lonely.

368
The staggering sound
Grew in all the directions
Giving me long pause.

369
Buzzing cicadas
Dazzle the night with their calls.
Lake stands alone now.

370
A divine brisk wind
Sends the peonies into
Hiding their petals.

371
The foggy silent
Night came up and bit me hard.
What happened there?

372
The temple tower,
Like a pillar of solid
Gold, standing aloof.

373
Wild geese fly their way
Into the dark of the night,
Into the heart's soul.

374
Agonizing heat
Attracted the various
Nighthawks to their den.

375
Once the moon goes down,
The night becomes itself again,
At river's bottom.

376
A straw basket stands
Next to the hearth near my bed,
Empty of all things.

377
Fireflies glow in the dark,
Giving everyone the taste
Of light fantastic.

378
I would like to use
That scarecrow's tattered clothes
In this nighttime frost.

379
Lonely silence.
A single cicada cries,
Sinking into stone.

380
Smoke blows all away.
The bamboo shoots gather it
And my chimney gloats.

381
Maiden flowers bloom,
Shedding their morning teardrops
Onto the forest floor.

382
Sick on my journey,
Only will my dreams wander
These desolate moors.

383
A cup of rice tea
Sits on the table softly,
And sips itself dry.

384
Buzzing with laughter,
The bee goes about his way.
Spring rain falls again.

385
From these many trees,
In salads, soups, everywhere
Cherry blossoms fall.

386
Gopher speaks to worm,
Meeting where none dare to go,
My dog discovers.

387
Twilight's red colors
Salute the day's end of days,
Nevermore to part.

388
Winter seclusion.
Out of the winter's snowstorms
The fire burns brightly.

389
Trout sleeping soundly
In deep pools of dark water.
Waking is difficult.

390
Fleas and mosquitos.
Bothersome without remorse,
Giving in to greed.

391
A splendid moonlight
Keeps the frogs from singing
And keeping me awake.

392
His unfortunate
Lover lost her brave battle
Without a worry.

393
Birthday becomes her.
And the flowers glow brightly
As the stars above.

394
The years first bright day
Wakens me, no one to see
Me but the rainbows.

395
Dragonflies moving.
Step aside for someone here
Who knows what they know.

396
Suddenly a storm
Shocks the Buddha into rage.
Angry without rest.

397
The unthinkable.
Events that transpire again,
Whenever bears come.

398
Snails charge into night
Without a care in sight.
My hut in the way.

399
After the sunset,
The darkness wraps its cold arms
Around my shoulders.

400
What to do when the
Calls of the night hawk tremble
In the windy woods?

401
Violets growing
Wild in the summer's sunlight.
Where do gardens go?

402
Scatter the seedlings,
For it matters not how far
Or what direction.

403
The lotus blossoms
Twinkle in the night's starlight,
Brightening my day.

404
Dancing monkeys leap
From the trees into my life,
Laughing as they do.

405
Little butterflies
Land on my fence look at me,
And I watch them go.

406
Scarecrow! It scares me
To never allow the birds that fly
Around it to land.

407
The crying willow,
With its tears striking the ground,
Flooding my garden.

408
Pathfinders need not
Find the only way to go.
But must find a way.

409
My old dog's head rests
On my lap where it belongs,
Forever it seems.

410
Into my garden,
The daffodils grow again,
And I ask not why.

411
Summer grasses.
All that remains of great men and
Imperial dreams.

412
Ring all the bells!
Never has arrived today,
And may soon be gone.

413
Seldom do my dogs
Leave my bedside anymore,
Since they are old too.

414
Beware of falcons,
For their claws easily grab
Anything that moves.

415
On a windy night,
Butterflies cannot even
Hover above me.

416
Deep in waters
Lie the patiently waiting
Jaws of predators.

417
The talons of eagles
Dig deeply into the backs
Of lesser mortals.

418
A black spider's web
Trembled on my hut waiting
For a passerby fly.

419
Nowhere but my hut
Does a bed seem natural
Enough to sleep in.

420
Seven days watching
Sent everyone scurrying
To birds without rest.

421
The vegetables
Grow in the meadow quietly,
While large swallows fly.

422
Hermit crab sideways . . .
Under a rock for safety
From a fisherman.

423
Beggars walk on pale
Improvised forgotten roads
With hollow desire.

424
A cloudburst above
Sends rain into my soup's dish.
No rice for today!

425
Wildflowers blooming.
Wildfires burning and smoking.
And I run away.

426
The degradations stiffened
Her grandchildren's
Backs, showing their predator's teeth.

427
His aggressive throne
Boldly gave him sickliness
From his beginning.

428
Their happiness
Severed when her collection
Rose to tempered heights.

429
The forest in smoke,
Burning its bridges behind
In the morning hours.

430
That great tall oak,
Indifferent to all blossoms,
Appears more noble.

431
A fire crackles loud
As everyone gathers round
For many stories.

432
Cucumber pudding
Only an arm's length away
Gives me an eye full.

433
Geese avoid dewdrops
And quarrel amongst themselves
About the world's rush.

434
Up on the mountain,
The meadows rest in the shade
Of the forests there.

435
Across the meadow
Two deer staring back at me
Waiting to wander.

436
Warriors turn back
When swallows plow far ahead
Into the night sky.

437
In the lake's shallows,
The spawning fish look up now,
Seeing me looking.

438
My front porch looks out
Over the shores of a lake,
Watching the fish jump.

439
The winter wind gave
Chase to the ravens above,
And sweeps by my gate.

440
Going from here to
There presents a problem of
Coming from here to there.

441
Making fun of the
Sparrows can force plum trees to
Forget who they are.

442
After his good friends
Encouraged my worthlessness,
I gave them my mind.

443
Umbrella shades my
Flowers in the hot summer.
Where is my shovel?

444
In the middle of
Carving a small statue of
Myself in mirrors.

445
The dust from a storm
Can wreck havoc on a
Small village people.

446
A weeping willow
Gives its best imitation of
Caring not the least.

447
The Buddha scowls
Whenever the anger grows.
Luckily for me.

448
Glory and wonder
Come but a small step away
From envy and more.

449
A lost child forgives
Our ringing the bell for her
From the village square.

450
Sliding into base,
Even a turtle knows that
Turning a blind eye.

451
Amazing graces.
Steep wilderness uncovered
Long entombed bodies.

452
Never count a wren out.
For each one knows the answer,
And treats it just right.

453
In my garden's blight
A swallow stands upright and
Waits for winter's come.

454
Pampas grass blew round,
Lightning struck the forest green,
And grandfather slept.

455
The icicles dripped,
And the snow melted slowly.
Spring gave us all hope.

456
Towering above
All who stand upright and tall,
The elm's grandeur calls.

457
Broadsided gophers
Dig deeper into the mud,
Escaping the view.

458
Bubbles in the pond
Give away a lonely frog
And a clue for flies.

459
From the dark shadows
Comes a creature that only
Knows of its future.

460
No fewer than mine,
The numbers of battles that
Signal my defeats.

461
Rice paper is blank,
Until a simple line finds
Its home on it.

462
Cold stands the river,
Ice in its bowels, and snow
On its flanks so cold.

463
Leaves on a tree limb
Blow in the wind of the night
Waking me from dreams.

464
Watching a worm wiggle
Its way from the ground,
Makes a robin watch me.

465
With dewdrops dripping,
I wish I somehow could wash
This perishing world.

466
On frozen rice fields,
Moving slowly on horseback,
My shadow creeps by.

467
This sunken temple
Should have its sad tale told only
By a clam digger.

468
With plum blossom scent,
Suddenly sun emerges
Along a mountain trail.

469
For reconciled
Lovers, the ladybugs were
Innocent again.

470

Without question now,
A bird's best friend is a seed
Lying on the ground.

471

A cuckoo cries,
And through a thicket of bamboo,
A late moon shines.

472

Breakfast enjoyed
The fine company of
Morning glories.

473

A lonely maple
Stands alone in the meadow
Waiting for nothing.

474

Seventeen sparrows
Stood in a row on a limb
And swallowed their pride.

475

Vermillion blossoms
Bless the meadows whenever
Light touches them.

476

A trumpeter's sound
Blasts through the quiet of the
Night and settles the fight.

477
Too few caterpillars
Bunch in the rice before me.
Butterflies coming!

478
Dreaming of dark skies,
A nesting meadowlark sings
Of prosperous times.

479
A world of dew,
And within each dewdrop,
A world of struggle.

480
How reluctantly
The bee emerges from down
Within the peony.

481
Now our bridge's length
Is quieted by flowers.
Like our snake-filled life.

482
Crossing the island
Comes a big black bear swearing
To never get caught.

483
Already frightened,
A forgotten skunk readies
His tail for a shot.

484

Nightingales warble
As the sunlight disappears
Into the waters.

485

The mighty sea gives
Shallow boats respite at night
To give sailors their sleep.

486

A skeleton tree
Stands on the horizon's edge
Like a lightning bolt.

487

Grasshoppers follow
Scents of wheat and green clover.
And robins follow them.

488

Talent knows no bounds
When hounds go hunting after
Gophers in the night.

489

The fruits of my trees
Lie at the feet of their trunks
Rotting in their skins.

490

Carnivorous bears
Often eat on the run from
Having to catch up.

491
In the dark of night,
Several finches gathered
Together for heat.

492
Rose petals turn yellow
As the moon glows full and bright,
The fallow field's blight.

493
Enthusiastic
Robins gliding through the air
Quickly transforming us.

494
Caught in a tangle,
A shrew threw her arms in air,
And made it all worse.

495
Lonely days and nights
Make suffering more able
To give up the ghost.

496
Bells ringing softly
A very long way from home
Strengthens my spirit.

497
Nightmarish shadows
Slither across my barn's wall
Giving me the creeps.

498

In the dark of night,
I wait until the moon goes
And then go alone.

499

Why does the ant hill
Stand so far away from me
And my ant swatter?

500

A bright comet came
Slipping into the night sky
Waking up my eyes.

501

Seven hawks above
Watch me for a sign below
That night will soon come.

502

Ask the winds that blow
What leaf on the tree
Will next be gone.

503

After killing
A spider, how lonely I feel
In the cold of night.

504

Spring buds to flowers,
Don't you risk another freeze?
Tell the weather no.

505
Glaciers melt to ponds.
Do not freeze again until
Winter makes its move.

506
On a mountain cliff,
Climbing toward the stars above
Gives me faint of heart.

507
Bamboo stalks stand high
Making shadows of the sky
Catching me aware.

508
Twelve monkeys stand
Looking at me in the lake,
Grieving for their souls.

509
Red sunset tonight.
Why do you stay so long
Making my heartache?

510
In the sky above,
Several finches abound,
Watching us below.

511
The seasonal rains
Along a nameless river.
Fear too has no name.

512

A lost summer's day
Moving the clouds past my
Window when nothing is found.

513

Locusts hum in tune
With summer's lost heated days
And in winter's frost.

514

Birds flying away,
And flying back again,
Never finding home.

515

Bluebirds in the sky,
Do not tell me that you won't,
Tell me that you will.

516

Vultures never wait,
But take their prey and turn it
Into food again.

517

Slender blades of grass
Underfoot, do bend and twist,
But never break.

518

Fallen red blossoms
From plum trees, burst into flame
Among the horse turds.

519
Herons fly away
When summer nights give sway
To tiresome winters.

520
Left at home alone
With nothing else to do,
A mouse runs past me.

521
Birds in captured skies,
Give me your talisman please,
So I can return.

522
Joyous holidays.
Give me your tempers without
Risk of losing them.

523
Peonies embrace
The karasaki pine tree.
Frogs leap into ponds.

524
After the mountains
Boldly wistful glaciers
Gave me boundaries.

525
A village pauper
Standing in the shade of an
Apple tree. Waiting.

526
Rainbow's glowing light
Fills me with joy and delight,
On this frightful night.

527
Isolated lake's
Reflected light and motion
For my sleepy self.

528
Along the river,
A priest arrives in white cloth,
Telling his stories.

529
The last trumpeter
Asks for a symbol of love
From everyone here.

530
Little yellow bugs
Stand on their hind legs looking
For what I don't know.

531
Spiders dancing slow
Beside the heat of a fire
And not biting me.

532
Just when the sermon
Has finally dirtied my ears.
The cuckoo!

533
Clinging to his bell,
He dozes so peacefully,
This new butterfly.

534
With the noon conch blown,
Those old rice planting songs
Are suddenly gone.

535
Praying for rainstorms,
Listening for thunders past,
Hoping the rice grows.

536
Tea by the river,
Faces of the puffer fish
In the blooming trees.

537
Peonies standing,
Watching the sun move across
Skies of immense size.

538
The thwack of an ax
In the heart of a thicket,
And a woodpecker's whack.

539
With a bitter wind,
A solitary monk bends
To words cut in stone.

540
Grandmother's watching
Her grandchildren play soccer.
A pepper tree calls!

541
Universe of grass
Hold both of my feet to earth
Forever after.

542
Stardust reveals its
Wondrous proclivities
To all who listen.

543
Catching a bluebird
Wanting to escape my grasp.
Letting him go now . . .

544
Branches of trees sag
Under the weight of the snow,
Waiting for sunlight.

545
Are you lecturing
Me about my heavy drink?
You mountain cuckoo.

546
Divine mystery
In these autumn leaves that fall
On stone Buddhas.

547
Forty-one pheasants
Standing in a field waiting,
Watching the sunset.

548
At the water's edge,
A frog leaps into the lake
Near where the fly fell.

549
Filled with sleep wrinkles,
Orchids show me how to live,
How to love, and die.

550
My ramshackle hut,
While plowing my fields into
Voices of insects.

551
The pot boils over
Into the fire below it,
And trouble's afoot.

552
Without a sound,
Munching young rice plants stalk
While caterpillars dine.

553
A single leaf falls,
Then suddenly another,
Stolen by the breeze.

554
The moon hides tonight,
Behind melancholy clouds,
Waiting to burst forth.

555
Katydids walking
Over my grave on a dark
Rainy day in spring.

556
Telltale signs of hawks
Appear whenever the eggs
Of wrens disappear.

557
To learn how to die,
Watch cherry blossoms, observe
Chrysanthemums.

558
A single yam leaf
Contains the entire life
Of a water drop.

559
Tadpoles convene in
Groups of five or more, ready
To grow into frogs.

560
Adventures begin,
When the afternoon wanes and
Black bears entertain.

561
With a broken wing,
The robin could barely fly.
Nurse him back to health.

562
Scattering blossoms,
Mattering much in the harsh
Choking of the mist.

563
Playing the flute
Makes the moon dance above me.
A bear listens too!

564
A shuttlecock reaches
The edge of its path toward me,
Even amidst starlight.

565
Music to my ears,
The never-ending joy of
Sounds spreading wonder.

566
The pheasant cries loud.
I do not object, for it
Makes my life pleasant.

567
Calligraphers caught
The robin and the eagle
Standing by the road.

568
Ducks cuddle their eggs,
Watching for signs that any
Dangers lie afoot.

569
On Buddha's birthday,
An orphaned boy will become
The temple's child.

570
You rice field maidens!
The only things not muddy,
Are the songs you sing.

571
The nightingale sings
In the perfect key of life.
Always happy birds.

572
The crow flies away
Across the rice field into
The moonless dark night.

573
The sky wears clouds of
Wind, making goblins with their
Morning glory's love.

574
Two bubbles together
Vanishing into nothing.
A flower blooms.

575
I killed an ant,
And realized my three children
Had been watching.

576
A sudden shower falls,
And naked am I riding
On a naked horse.

577
Shorter summer nights,
Without a home in this world,
Every evening rain.

578
When the sky turns red,
The sun has turned its back on
Us and falls asleep.

579
Duckweed blooms on the
Earthworm's song, my rice cake
Stuck to the hunted bird.

580
A lovely thing to see
Through the paper windows.
A hole the clouds.

581
Silly red magpies
Caught in a storm, flying
In a darkened sky.

582
Extending from the
Pampas grass far from my home,
Five feet of snow.

583
Over many hills
Lies the everlasting meaning
Of the eagles soaring.

584
Buddha's wildflowers
Give the billowing clouds their
Sovereign test of love.

585
A giant firefly flies
That way, this way, that way,
And it passes by.

586
Covered with flowers,
I'd like to die instantly
In this dream of yours.

587
At the over-matured
Sushi, the Master is
Full of regret.

588
Won't you come and see,
The loneliness of one leaf
From the kiri tree?

589
Poverty's child
Starts to grind the rice,
And gazes at the moon.

590
Clouds appear and bring
Men a chance to rest
From looking at the moon.

591
As isolated
Apricots fall, evolution
Provides its glories.

592
Our scrupulous cat
Clarified its bitterness
With threats of fancy.

593
Fireworks above me,
Lighting the way for strangers
Seeking new places.

594
Tripping over limbs,
I walk into the forest
Limping over grass.

595
Never mind the store,
Its life is nevermore,
Or so the stranger said.

596

Twelve ordinary doves
Stand in the meadow eating.
The red fox watches.

597

Sparrows wept upon
The mountains pine breeze,
Wafting over the meadow's grass.

598

Red sunsets portend
That rain must fall the morrow,
And test our waking.

599

Glaciers hug it like
Beaver coats might like to do.
Mount Fuji at night.

600

The water spills from
Rocks above the lake and gives
Turtles a shower.

601

A pig's snout stuck out
From the slats of my white fence
Snorting his wishes.

602

A pale rider came
Upon a strange looking man
And offered him luck.

603
A tiny spider
Glides along its web trying
To find a fly there.

604
Forest of green trees,
A fire comes rushing at you.
What say you now?

605
Just to say the word
Home, makes one seem so
Pleasantly cool again.

606
The mountain glacier
Hung like an emerald caught
Fighting for its life.

607
Lightning flashing sky
From a thunderhead holding
Rain back from my soul.

608
The New Year arrived
In complete simplicity,
And a deep blue sky.

609
Down by the river,
An egret stood on one leg,
A flash of silver.

610

A brilliant white dusk
Gave the sky and darkened clouds
A special taste of love.

611

In crying, the cicada
Gives no sign foretelling
How soon it will die.

612

Over the wintry forest,
Winds howl in rage
With no leaves blowing.

613

Old silent waters.
A frog jumps into the pond,
Splash, then silence again.

614

Brightest moon, is it true
That you too must
Pass in a hurry?

615

For love or for hate,
You swat a fly and
Offer it to an ant.

616

Too many daffodils
For the garden to hold them.
I noticed a wren.

617
Gloomy weather told
Of ice and snow at higher
Places in the hills.

618
Tender morsels of
Bamboo shoots striving for sky
As the spring rain falls.

619
White light gives the night
Special tastes of glory and
Never ever ends.

620
A wood beetle walked
Around the bark of a tree
To see what it was.

621
In my hidden hut,
No teeth left in my mouth,
But good luck abounds.

622
Blue herons arise
From the waters of the lake.
Fish are happy, too.

623
Ponds with frogs agree
That life is but one part of
Everything at all.

624

A world of paths,
And if the cherry blossoms,
It simply blossoms.

625

Dipping my toes in
Water so deep and cold that
Frogs leap from the lake.

626

Hiding my snow boots,
Makes it all the harder to
Find my way home.

627

Suddenly thunder
Pounds on my hut from above.
The muskrat hides, too.

628

Where can I go now
To settle my hunger for
Rice cakes and pudding?

629

As the grand old trees
Are marked for felling, the birds
Build their new spring nests.

630

Salt never fails to
Make the snow melt or the water
Not for me to drink.

631

A brown forest rat
Wanders across the garden
Looking for a snack.

632

The terraced mountain
Gives up its soul to harvest.
The rice for our souls.

633

White mice in white rice,
Sneakily grinding their teeth,
Living beyond means.

634

Along the river
Banks comes a single raccoon
Looking forward now.

635

A shy nightingale
Postures himself for debate
With the dandelion.

636

The distant mountains
Are reflected in the eye
Of a dragonfly.

637

Casting the line off,
A boatman strings out his line
And fish disappear.

638
After several
Leaps toward the fountain, a frog
Captures a dead fly.

639
Before the autumn winds,
Even the shadows of mountains
Shudder and tremble.

640
The wilderness weighed
More than all the world's many
Short frosty tempers.

641
Reeds in the water
Bend in the wake of a wind.
Never to return.

642
The green slime of mold
Hides the deep poaching of worms,
Or their brave cousins.

643
Seaweed floats ashore
When storms cease to pound
Winter's angry energy.

644
The fireflies blinking
Gave us a night of surprise.
So the frogs told us!

645

No one could figure
The awful cost of the storm.
But the bear unconcerned.

646

Once protected moon,
Surrendered her ideas
Of the innocent.

647

The boats at harbor
Rest their sails amid the winds,
And the gulls resist.

648

Thus spring begins, old
Stupidities repeat,
New errs invented.

649

None but the lonely
Have in their natures the sense
Of what they have not.

650

Trees bent by the wind
Holler to me to come and
Put them back again.

651

Punctuated words
Give rise to unordered lives,
Watching worms burrow.

652
Where does the badger
Go when he disappears at
Night in the forest?

653
My cat crouches in
The meadow and watches wrens.
The bear notices.

654
Just beyond the gate,
A neat yellow hole.
Someone pissed in the snow!

655
Fasting all day long,
A turtle slowly walks down.
A swim in the lake.

656
All of a sudden,
Three kittens arrive at once,
Fighting for their milk.

657
Spiders lay their eggs
Where no one can find them hid,
And scrape them away.

658
A winter fly
I caught and finally freed,
The cat quickly ate.

659
Once in a lifetime,
Witness a wave crashing loud
Against the shoreline.

660
Ice spread on the road
Makes walking hard for my
Friends without their sandals.

661
Suddenly, as if
Brought back from the edge of
Death, the dog barks again.

662
Alone in the forest,
A magpie screams for mercy,
And gets his way.

663
An old ragged dog
Sleeps soundly on a park bench
Waiting for the night.

664
Wisest older owl
Sits on a branch waiting for
Something to happen.

665
Fox outwits cowards,
Chases them towards the raccoon,
Who keeps them from harm.

666

Willows bend their limbs
Downward toward the lowest Ground. Gophers reach their
ends.

667

Out my wide window,
The wood thrush seems to smile at
The vulture there alone.

668

Gentle fiddleheads
Sprout like no characters
In earthly paradise.

669

Even disappearing tip
Of tail is still nothing
But a snake's body.

670

Robin red breast,
How did you get your color
From the nightingale?

671

Fortunately the
Eagle was last in line for
Dinner that evening.

672

Figurative flutes
Defended their acoustic
Impressions of life.

673
Shadows from a lingering sun
Blur into dusk.
Falling cherry petals!

674
Leaves twirling in wind,
Bend the light into colors
Where the badger sleeps.

675
Fallible people,
Give in to their foibles, and
Try to make amends.

676
Falling down into
The meadow this afternoon,
The butterfly rests.

677
The world's beautiful
Passengers wandered alone
Along the highway.

678
At last I am leaving.
In rainless skies a cool moon,
Pure is my heart.

679
Since time began,
The dead alone know peace.
Life is but melting snow.

680
Sleeping on a cot,
Watching an old spider sleep
In its web of death.

681
Tender winds above the
Melting snow's many kinds
Of suffering.

682
The chair where I sit
Gives me a small view of you
Staring at the lake.

683
Water collides with
Sunken dams and tired beavers.
Lightning braves the skies.

684
Wisps of clouds sail
Across the deep blue windows
That reflect my sky.

685
As the snow piles high,
The gopher crawls to safety
Up a dead tree trunk.

686
Battles of beetles,
Fighting with armored bodies,
Never won or lost.

687
High above my head
A swooping hawk kills for lunch.
But he misses me.

688
A journey of no return.
The wanderer's sack
Is bottomless.

689
A sleepy dolphin
Speeds through the waters in
Search of her enemies.

690
Snows of yesterday
That fell like cherry petals,
Is water once again.

691
Fields dying,
The underside of grasses frozen,
The hour of my death!

692
On a journey ill,
My dreams go wandering
Over withered fields.

693
Earth and metal,
Although my breathing ceases,
Time and tide go on.

694
The deep slush of boots,
Collect in the night air and
Never give it a thought.

695
Icicles hang from
The roof of my hut above,
Testing my honor.

696
Snow stands deep around
My hut and watches me sleep.
Caution tells me why.

697
A single robin
Lights on a candle near water
Causing confusion.

698
Winds blow flags around,
Cautioning everyone here
To stop wondering.

699
Capable people
Watch as the storm clouds gather,
Waiting for rain.

700
Orange red sunsets,
Swift holidays recruited,
Late conversations.

701
Silvery moon shines
Over the meadow where snakes
Crawl their way home.

702
Old enables new,
Whether crows, deer, or fishes,
In air, land, or sea.

703
A regal swan floats near,
Barely touching the water.
Give me your honor!

704
The resolution
Of many of life's problems
Comes at severe cost.

705
Garbage collected
Behind his shed, where many
Things got put instead.

706
Since morning glories
Hold my well bucket hostage,
I beg for water.

707
A mosquito buzzes
Every time the flowers
Of honeysuckle fail.

708
First autumn morning.
The mirror you stare into
Shows my father's face.

709
Large hogs come calling
Through winter fences that bind
Their madness to all.

710
Now the bridge afar
Is silenced by strangers,
Like our struggled life.

711
The beautiful frog
Divinified all his life
By his bravery.

712
Ashes! My burned hut.
But wonderful the cherry
Blooming on the hill.

713
Of the heavy temple bell,
A moon sloth folded into.
Sleep sits still!

714
Candlestick in hand,
He strolls through the garden,
Grieving over spring.

715

Cherry blossoms fall
On watery rice-plant beds.
Stars in the moonlight.

716

An evening orchid,
Hidden in its scent.
The flower's whiteness glows.

717

White dew before dawn,
Over the potato field
Is the Milky Way.

718

It's fall in the evening,
When no one is walking
Along this road.

719

Here, where a thousand
Captains swore their conquest,
Tall grass their monument.

720

Now that eyes of hawks
In dusky light are darkened,
Chirping of the quail.

721

Footfalls in the snow,
Soft and deep his shoes sink down,
Making trails of holes.

722
Geese flying south
To avoid winter snowfall
And windy dark nights.

723
Temple bells die away,
But the blossoms remain.
A perfect evening.

724
Shadows in the dusk.
Providing a place to hide
Before darkness comes.

725
On a withered branch,
A crow has landed here.
Nightfall in autumn.

726
Shoveling manure
To spread it far on the earth,
Granting the rice life.

727
Tremble on my grave mound.
In time, my cries will be
Heard in this autumn wind.

728
Under my tree,
Roof slanting lines of April rain
Separating to drops.

729
Songs from the willow,
Bending in the nervous winds,
Waiting for its mate.

730
In the darkest night,
He heard the sound of thunder
Rumbling its way home.

731
The banana tree
Blown by winds pours raindrops
Into my bucket.

732
On the polished surface
Of the divine glass,
Chaste with flowers of snow.

733
Exhausted, I sought
A country inn, but found
Wisteria in bloom.

734
Preoccupation.
Beauties of all tomorrows
As everyone saw.

735
Even that old horse
Is something to see on this
Snow-covered morning.

736

The first fallen snow
Is barely enough to bend
The jonquil leaves.

737

Silence can be lonely,
For a single cicada cries,
Sinking into ground.

738

Skunks lift their tails
To give you a smell of hell
And keep you away.

739

The petals tremble
On the yellow mountain rose.
Roar of the rapids.

740

When had he lost it?
He couldn't remember that.
But did it matter?

741

Tinted light of dawn
Makes day seem welcome to all
Except porcupines.

742

Petal by petal,
Yellow mountain roses fall.
The sound of rapids.

743

In a back alley,
Two angry sparrows conspired
To find his lost coin.

744

Silenced are the sounds
Of dogs barking, cats whining,
Butterflies flying.

745

Where do they keep it?
The shopkeeper asked his friend,
Never minding his thoughts.

746

Deep in a dark cave,
An old man hid his findings
From everyone else.

747

Looking carefully,
A shepherd's herd is crawling
Under the fence.

748

Along a mountain road.
Somehow it tugs at my heart.
A wild violet.

749

On a mountain top,
An eagle sat eagerly
Awaiting his prey.

750

In the lily pond,
Two rusty colored wrens sat
Speaking of friendship.

751

Rice sits in water
Pointing its finger upwards,
Waiting for the rains.

752

In a deep earth rut,
The eggs of a robin lay
Waiting for thunder.

753

Three knocks at my door.
Who comes at this time of night
Catching me off guard?

754

Flying across sand,
A seagull called toward the man,
Hoping to fool him.

755

Castles lie quiet,
Ruins of their former selves,
Waiting to crumble.

756

Dreams of golden hens
Laying their big golden eggs
In the palm of your hand.

757
I cannot believe
What grandeur the winter's snow
Has given to us.

758
Fire embers grow dim
When the wind blows cold at night
And more wood required.

759
A flurry of snow
Attracted a stray bluebird
Hoping to catch some.

760
The bells rang loudly,
Welcoming the winter's past.
What do you say bear?

761
Eagles fly higher
Than the sky, and catch the sun
Before it sails to me.

762
Cautious meadowlarks
Stood in their nests in the field,
Waiting for night to come.

763
The sunlight between the clouds
Sliced through the dark sky
Like pointed fingers.

764
Gourds of melons gone,
Lay beside my grandfather
Like billiard balls.

765
Sleeping brings good things
To those who do not have dreams,
And those who cannot.

766
Lying under the sun
On a hot summer's dry day
Waiting for nothing.

767
Cranky robins scream
Of all the injustices
They've seen today.

768
Never lost for words,
The gambler played his cards.
The bear said, after all.

769
A cloud in the sky
Slowly moved toward the
Mountain waiting to catch it.

770
Bury your husbands
Under the earth, but be careful,
Wait until they're dead.

771

Too many crows here.
Never a good thing for fields,
Because of the seeds.

772

A warbler warbled
Softly behind the garden.
Singing him to sleep.

773

Before your children
Interrupted, I dreamt that
They had my wallet.

774

Climbing up the hill,
A young man set his sights high
For the eagle there.

775

Angry sparrows screech,
When bluebirds come calling them,
Especially in spring time.

776

Double rainbows rise
Over the mountain crests,
With four golds not two.

777

My hut never heats,
Except when it's hot outside,
And cold when it's cold.

778
Deep rains soften the earth,
Make beautiful mud when deep,
And walking a mess.

779
My soul yearns for love.
But it will not come when asked,
Only when it's not.

780
Fistfuls of berries,
Lying in wait as you walk,
Trying not to wink.

781
Too few able men
Gathered together tonight,
Watching the moon glow.

782
Caution rides the wind
Whenever doves fall to earth.
A man with a gun!

783
A long dance tonight,
For the rice will grant us all
Never ending wonder.

784
A ghost in the shed
Has caused me to relinquish
My hold on my mind.

785
Silence cries to me,
Lying its head down upon
My soft shoulders.

786
Dewdrops do collect
Whenever it's cold and wet,
And gets in your shoes.

787
Don't let the cherries
Bask in the sun for so long
They become berries.

788
Where the horses roam,
Several horsemen follow,
Tending their white sheep.

789
A sliver of moon
Smiles at me from the night sky.
From ear to ear it laughs.

790
Calico cats sleep,
Waking only when mothers
Call for their children.

791
Never forget snails.
They make many mistakes when
Crossing busy roads.

792
Chestnuts alone,
Disappearing into mist
Where squirrels roam.

793
Harkening a toad
Brings ominous calling.
A loon on the lake.

794
The sea touches the
Horizon forever gone
From my seeing it.

795
Knee deep in snowfall,
An old man watches his feet
Sink into the white flakes.

796
Butterflies shimmer
In a late summer morning,
Basking in the sun.

797
A leafless tree stands
Motionless before my horse,
Pointing toward the way.

798
Foxy wrens take time
To criticize others
That criticize them.

799
Fires in the dark night
Glow like suns scattered around
In our somber tomb.

800
A dead sparrow
Lands in the path where I walk.
Should I pick it up?

801
Sinister horses
Sidling their way with riders,
Chasing their shadows.

802
The color of light,
Depends on the line of sight
That brings it here.

803
Under the table,
A marble has found its way,
Rolling from my sight.

804
The drum beats loudly
Over the meadows and hills,
Keeping me awake.

805
The winds of Mount Fuji.
I've turned on my fan.

A gift from Edo.

806

The first cold shower.
Even the monkey seems to want
A little coat of straw.

807

A light breeze touches
The very essence of my heart.
Never letting go.

808

The pond still and cold!
A frog has jumped from shore.
The splash can be heard.

809

Now then, let's go out
And enjoy the snow,
Until I slip and fall.

810

Another year has gone.
A traveler's shade on my head.
Straw sandals on my feet.

811

Snow turns to deep slush
As it melts around my hut.
Losing sleep over it.

812

In the wake of a
Storm, animals rush toward water

Hoping to keep dry.

813
My grand daughter's nose
Points toward the heaven where it
Originated.

814
Studying forests,
The old man sleeps in the well,
Waiting for water.

815
A stick stands lonely,
Watching the garden growing
Forever after.

816
Dark shadows engulf
Me from the mountains afar.
Night comes early here.

817
With seldom-heard voice,
A sheepherder stands aside
And lets his sheep pass.

818
Glowing in the night,
A firefly turns off his light,
And sleeps just like me.

819
Leaving a long trail
Of consequential breadcrumbs,

The hiker resists.

820

A message arrives.
Sent by someone far away,
And received by me.

821

At the very top,
A climber stops for a view
Of the wilderness.

822

Information comes
In the forms of many things.
Like a dog barking.

823

A single flower
Points toward the sun as it does
Whenever it wants.

824

The thunderclouds slip
Silently by the mountains
As the deer eats grass.

825

At rainbow's ending,
A small mouse struggles along,
Hoping for better things.

826

Deep in the earth, a
Worm crawls slowly around the
Roots of my peach tree.

827

Staring at the moon
Does one no good at all
During the daytime.

828

Along a solemn path
A lonely man walks softly
Hoping for my guilt.

829

Diving into earth,
A wary rat seeks just one
Route out of death.

830

Too few sparrows now,
For I cannot find even
One standing alone.

831

With every gust of wind,
A butterfly changes its place
On the willow.

832

Sick of the journey,
Only my dreams will wander
These desolate moors.

833

With just seconds left,
The snake prefers to wiggle
Down the hole to hell.

834
Things to be forgotten.
The pot where this flower blooms
This fine spring day.

835
In my house with me,
All the mice and fireflies
Agree together.

836
What a world this is,
When lotus flowers are plowed
Down into the ground.

837
Come let us see
All the beautiful flowers of this
Sorrowful world.

838
Ungraciously, under
A great soldier's empty helmet,
A cricket sings.

839
Searching for dinner,
A titmouse wanders over
And catches a cold.

840
Where six wrens gather,
Sixteen owls watching sit,
Wondering why.

841
The glint off snow.
High on the mountain glaciers
A lonely bear climbs.

842
Afternoon winds blow,
Causing a chicken hawk to
Turn back in wonder.

843
Sliding out of sight,
A snake slithers its way towards
The tadpoles swimming.

844
Sixty-two runners
Cross the finish line ahead
Of the turtle mouse.

845
Reflecting water
Doubles the number of stars
On the waves at sea.

846
Why anticipate?
If you must give my name to
Them, do so with honor.

847
The sweet smell of rose
Accompanies me to town
Where peaches await.

848
Buddha rings a bell.
The forest pays attention.
The mountains alone.

849
A soft rain falls,
Landing on the roof of my hut,
Tender as the day.

850
The dazzling moon
Brightens my night when it's full
Towering above.

851
Gray hairs being plucked.
And from below my pillow,
A cricket singing.

852
Secretly at night,
A worm under the moon
Crawls into a chestnut.

853
But for a woodpecker
Tapping at a post, no sound
At all in the house.

854
With a warbler for
A soul, it sleeps peacefully
On mountain willow.

855
Autumn approaches.
And the heart begins to dream
Of four tatami rooms.

856
Darkness hides evil
From anyone seeing it
Crawling away far.

857
Very exciting.
Yet after awhile so sad.
Cormorant fishing.

858
Seas slowly darken,
With the wild duck's plaintive cry
Growing faintly white.

859
A large beaver swims
Toward my hut on the shore line
Where I'm eating lunch.

860
A mountain pheasant's cry
Fills me with fond longing
For my father and mother.

861
My eyes follow
Until the bird who was lost at sea
Finds a small island.

862
The village so old.
There's not a single house
Without a persimmon tree.

863
The rice wine reflects
My face in its mirrored glass.
Where did my lines go?

864
Wet with morning dew,
And splotched with mud,
The melon looks especially good.

865
Searching storehouse eaves,
Rapt in plum blossom smells,
The mosquito sings.

866
When will they stop him
From grinding his rice into
Sauce for his gander?

867
Even these long days
Are not nearly long enough
For the skylarks to sing.

868
The shapes of large clouds,
Makes me think of faraway
Places and people.

869
Drinking morning tea,
The monk is peaceful,
And the chrysanthemum blooms.

870
All the more I wish to see,
In those blossoms at the dawn,
The face of god!

871
Selection of rice
Comes to my table at night.
The dog comes running.

872
Gifts from the mountain.
Snow on the ground, water, and
Fire in my stove.

873
Today's the day of
Reckoning, with the hornet
That's biting my soul.

874
The curious mouse
Struggles from its underground
Nest and looks around.

875
The urn full of soup
Boiling brightly on the stove.
Why does the mouse sit?

876
In the morning light
Everything seems brighter still
Then when last I saw.

877
Music to my ears.
For my heart and my soul,
But never for my feet.

878
The granite canyon
Sinks down toward the lake at its
Depths, waiting for me.

879
Walking under trees
Shades my head from the
Sunlight. Come get me old man.

880
Castles in the sky
Float idly by the meadow,
Making the rice dance.

881
A lone cloud drifts by,
Shading my old bones from the
Sun at last, old bear.

882
A herd of cattle
Wander into my garden.
Where are my fences?

883
Salvage the daylight.
Store it under your bed sheet,
And catch it at night.

884
Swimming beneath the
Water gives a different
View of the night sky.

885
A moonbeam crosses
In front of my face as it
Fits into my pocket.

886
Far in the heavens,
A particular star shines
Light on everyone.

887
In far away lands,
Young men gather the fruits from
Trees, and feed the earth.

888
Cancel the wedding,
The old man said, wondering
If he'd said it right.

889
The young muskrats
Run about underfoot, waiting
For their mother.

890
The fleas bother dogs
And dogs bother fleas as well.
Strange as it may seem.

891
Watching everything
Go by, is one of the traits
That grandfathers have.

892
Frail old man sits still,
Lighting his pipe and drinking
Tea from a large cup.

893
The tall apple tree
Lends its fruit to all that wait.
Even the scarecrow.

894
Because their yearning
For the wilderness alone,
They consumed berries.

895
Why do the goblets
Always seem to stand empty
When I've just filled them?

896
The rivers collide,
As they work themselves down the
Mountain in the rain.

897
This day of all days,
Writes the poet in his sleep,
As the nighthawk watches.

898
Wandering around,
An old man watches his life
Passing him aground.

899
Wrestling with robins
Made grandfather's habits stop
Seeking the lost rice.

900
The flycatcher took
All the undeniably
Profitable fish.

901
With each gust of wind,
Butterflies alter their perches
On the willow's branch.

902
In the third decade,
A tired old weeping willow
Lets down its green hair.

903
Winds blow heavy
When winter storms bring the
Snow and powder my hut.

904
Bare feet on cold floors
Brings out the best in lovers,
For nothing is lost.

905
Seventy years times
Seventy makes for a dire
Conviction of life.

906
Not long enough for
The skylark, but for the whole
Day, we sang and sang.

907
Gather the fruits of life,
And put them where they belong.
In your new garden.

908
Win some, lose many,
The woodpecker says to his
Friends and enemies.

909
Trees bending in wind,
Reach down to pick a flower,
And tell me good day.

910
Deep in the waters,
A coil of snakes readies for
Its revolution.

911
Who hoots at me now,
And gives its last hoot tonight?
Is it the hoot owl?

912
Granite mountains
Stand above me towering,
Giving me their shade.

913
Dead flowers suddenly
Burst into bloom again, now
That he's plowed his field.

914
Taking its fill of fruit,
A harbinger of fate wanders
By to say hello.

915
Death rides a gray horse,
Out from the sunset, into
My life, without hate.

916
A late evening crow
Of deep autumn longing,
Suddenly cries out.

917
As the spring breeze blows,
All according to Buddha,
Rushes go to seed.

918
Robins scolded my
Satisfied afterthoughts, by
Chattering their minds.

919
Interpretations
Are the backbone of the elm,
Always standing firm.

920
A faraway lake
Glimmers in the summer's sun,
Waiting for the rain.

921
Rice pudding is nice,
Especially when it comes
After my night's meal.

922
Seven daffodils
Struggle toward the summer sky,
Hoping to glimpse God.

923
Buddha offers the
Morning glory mosquitoes
And persimmon drops.

924
Ginger tea at night,
Makes my heart slumber as I
Fall asleep soundly.

925
In my line of sight,
A towering monument
Gives me lots of pause.

926
The faces of hills,
Turn toward my hut in winter,
Giving white visions.

927
Next in line stood a
Wandering bug in search of
Wild entertainment.

928
A shadow itself
Walks across the fall meadow
Imagining me.

929
You nasty bold terns
Living downwind from my cave.
The black bear yawning.

930
Stealing a chance to
Fill my glass with berry juice.
Why do robins watch?

931
Forgive the black snake,
For it knows not what it does
But what it does not.

932
The red dahlia.
Soft on the outside petals
Hard on the inside.

933
A neighbor's garden
Sits next to my fence with its
Grapes ready to eat.

934
Dewdrops on grass,
As in frosting on sweet cakes
When birthdays arrive.

935
Frogs singing tonight,
From the depths of the pond reeds,
Coy quietly drift.

936
Powerful rewards,
Make northern lights colliding
With vibrations.

937
Rice cakes and spring rains,
Along with the pampas grass,
Geese flying south.

938
A grasshopper jumps
From spot to spot in the grass,
Never knowing why.

939
Plum blossoms knowing
The bee's secret give way, for
Next the season comes.

940
Whether islands not,
They still stand in the waters,
Waiting for winter.

941
The lonely hermit
Dwelled but for seconds today.
The foxtails listen.

942
Why do grasshoppers
Sing like choirs as they do?
Is it protective?

943
Clouds gathered high
Piling up onto each other
For a great storm.

944
A rock's solid place,
Should never be displaced,
Unless by great force.

945
Fog drifts across lakes,
Moves over the green meadows,
But stops at mountains.

946
Reeds in the water
Move with the tide, but the moon
Takes the credit.

947
Moonrise over mountains
In the blackest of the night,
Lighting our windows.

948
Curious that the
Blackbird never seems to fly.
He stands on my roof.

949
From the rain shower,
All the lucky flowers come
Back from their nightmares.

950
Staggering around,
He promised himself never
To swim it again.

951
Unlucky horses
Maintain their poise and postures
To pull the wagons.

952
Late blooming roses
Give up their smells for us,
Through five feet of snow.

953
The cicadas chirp
For all to hear and follow
Their regular songs.

954
Sadly, the muskrat
Pretends he is drowning in
The lake behind me.

955
A doe wrestled her way
Out from the belly of her
Mother today.

956
A potbelly stove
Pours out the smoke into sky
Leaving me breathless.

957
Peeking in windows,
A pauper begs for his food,
But none comes his way.

958
On my arms and legs
Come butterflies and shadows,
Wings and peregrines.

959
With the evening breeze,
The water laps against
The heron's leg.

960
Fireworks and fireflies
Do not have much in common,
Except the word fire.

961
The thorny hedge bends
With devastating results.
My stammering song!

962
Along the right path,
A man makes his choice of life.
In what direction?

963
Past the wilderness,
A mountain range dwells with its
Staggering heights shorn.

964
The bright moon reflects
Itself in the pond below.
A frog laughs at me.

965
Forsaken, the man
Walks with his back to the lake
Towards my window.

966
Whenever I count
The bushels of rice in my
Hut, it comes out wrong.

967
White the heat rising
From mountains and meadow's
Glen, as steam from kettles.

968
An eagle stands proud
On the point of my fence gate
Watching me watch him.

969
Fourteen blackbirds land
Square in the back of my house
Ready to make amends.

970
Lovely white heron,
Standing alone in the pond,
Where the lilies grow.

971
Every day's a test
Of whether life's good or bad
And it's always both.

972
Down towards the river
Lives an old man capable
Of dying today.

973
He picked up a rock
And threw it at the gopher
Eating his garden.

974
My wind chimes blowing
In the winter weather cold,
Letting me know how.

975
Within the quietness
Of a lull in visitors around
Appears the peony flower.

976
Summer nights ending so soon?
While on the river shallows,
A sliver of moon remains.

977
Laughter and sadness
Are two of the same creatures.
Both sides of a coin.

978
Living life anew
Rewards the man who gives it
All away today.

979
Along distant paths,
I came across the shadow
Of my grandfather.

980
Flowers descended
From the enjoined freezing of
The temples and bells.

981
Clouds drifted toward him,
And terrified the beggar's
Angry moments.

982
Your lively partner
Gave flowers to me over
My high window ledge.

983
The slightest movement
Made the ground shake when
Thunder claps the heavens.

984
Dire predictions made,
Gave the hornet a chance to
Find another place.

985
How the brighter moon
Influenced the yesterdays
Of oblivion.

986
Go to the meadow,
Cries the maddening hornet
To my grandfather.

987
A placated mouse
Looked over at me while I sat
Expecting dessert.

988
Exasperation
Made everyone stand rigid,
Expecting surprise.

989
On top of my hut,
A crow pecks on my roof slats.
What are you doing?

990
My pasture gives me
Pleasure watching the horses
Eating the grasses.

991
Mushrooms poke their heads
Above the soft earth's caress,
After the sun sets.

992
Before the white
Chrysanthemum, the scissors
Hesitate a second.

993
I cannot believe
That worms use the ground to
Live, and I the surface.

994
The hole in the clouds
Gave the sun a chance to shine,
Even for a moment.

995
The first snow.
Just enough to bend
The leaves of the daffodils.

996
Through a thick growth
Of bamboo, a cuckoo cries as
The moon shines forth.

997
The golden grasses
Whip in the summer's windy
Afternoon's moment.

998
A rice field guards my
House from water-dreaming Thugs, and gives me my
dreams.

999
This bright harvest moon
Keeps me walking all night long
Around the little pond.

1000
The frog's new tonsils
Gave his voice a resonance
That stole the day away.

1001
The fog enshrouds me
Like a bear might a big hug
And then lets me go.

1002

Winter solitude.
In a world of one color,
The sound of wind.

1003

The bee emerges
From deep within the peony.
Departs reluctantly.

1004

A palace seaside
Sake makes the cat's coat gleam.
A raccoon no more.

1005

Along the mountain road,
Somehow it tugs on my heart.
A wild violet.

1006

Snow remains on the
Mountain slopes, misty on
An evening in spring.

1007

Everything that was,
Has vanished from my aged heart,
Leaving not a trace.

1008

Its house abandoned,
The garden has become
Home to butterflies.

1009
Until the morrow,
I shall not wake again nor
Ever give it thought.

1010
Sadness prevails when
More than one partakes of its
Tempting fate and sorrow.

1011
For coolness it rivals
The water's depths.
These gray autumn skies.

1012
The temple bell stops.
But the sounds keep coming
Out of the flowers.

1013
My grandfather's watch
Has taken a turn for the
Worse it seems today.

1014
Lotus blossoms bloom with
Never ending pungent life.
The frog leaps the more.

1015
Wood chopping in the
Distance, dancing sparks and
Chips, flying in the maelstrom.

1016
Walking on the shore
Makes me lonely for a mate.
Where am I going?

1017
In the blossoms shade,
As in the Noh drama,
A traveller sleeps.

1018
From all these trees,
In salads and soups everywhere,
Cherry blossoms fall.

1019
The dew sits on leaves
Waiting patiently for me
To look at it shine.

1020
Kaleidoscopic
Winter storms placate the
Once fierce summer sun.

1021
A lovely spring night
Suddenly vanished while we
Watched cherry blossoms.

1022
Never cross a finch.
It returns to bite your skin.
Not fun and painful.

1023
Towards the sun's way,
Hollyhocks turn to it
Through the rains of May.

1024
When the lightning stops,
When thunders cease sounding,
How deep the rain falls.

1025
Temple bells fade.
Cherry blossoms remain.
A blessed evening.

1026
The sun emerges suddenly,
Walking a mountain trail
With plum blossom scent.

1027
Over the ruins of a
Shrinea chestnut tree,
A candle still lifts.

1028
Fuji stands so high,
The clouds gather around it,
Staying there for night.

1029
Down near the valley,
Two dozen men prepare the
Fire for deposition.

1030
Her abiding love
Interrupted wolf and fox
For the swallow's call.

1031
The sky changed color.
How do you feel about the
Eagle that flies high?

1032
Along the lake's shore,
A covey of doves twitter,
With nothing to do.

1033
How can turtles bathe,
When the water's so dirty
And my feet so wet?

1034
Snow interrupted
Winter's crown for the lesson.
Thankful whippoorwills.

1035
Cutting off my hair
Gives freedom to my thoughts and
Celebrations for you!

1036
Welcome daffodils.
Did you come to see me blink?
Or not see you coming?

1037
Waiting for the snow.
Following the generous
Gifts from Buddha's heart.

1038
A proud persimmon
Hung from the branch for as long
As it took me to grab it.

1039
The crease in the earth
Had a stream running through it.
Going out to sea.

1040
On the frozen lake,
Two geese ski along nicely
Marking the soft ice.

1041
A sparrow fell down
From the sky and asked to die.
But I wouldn't let it.

1042
Water dripped from my
Roof, asking me to tell it
When to stop raining.

1043
A long trail followed
The river up the mountain.
Taking its own time.

1044
Up above my life,
A father waits for me to
Give away my soul.

1045
River of stars dealt
My temper a severe blow,
And a calm rainstorm.

1046
A soft warm wind blows.
The flowers in the meadow
Wave to me quietly.

1047
The gopher looked sad.
Waiting for me to kill it.
I didn't want to.

1048
The curtained window
Glowed brightly in moonlight,
Saving its best show.

1049
A pink daffodil
Lying on the lakeside beach,
Looked at me today.

1050
Twice on the same day,
A crow dived into my hut.
What to do raven?

1051
An ugly black bear
Crawls upon a mountain crest
Resting for a time.

1052
Too few meadowlarks
Calling in the evening's air.
Why do you not sleep?

1053
Windows in my hut
Shimmer in the summer sun,
Waiting for nightfall.

1054
The mouse in my hat
Struggles to get loose before
The hat's on my head.

1055
Bending in the wind,
Several trees send hopeful
Messages to me.

1056
A dry streambed stops
At my garden's gate in fall.
Waiting for the rains.

1057
A small riverlet
Dribbles by my feet today.
Where goes tomorrow?

1058

A big black bear stands
Staring at me from afar.
What do you want bear?

1059

Twinkling stars above
Travel across the night sky.
Where do you go then?

1060

Can spring be far away?
Waiting in its secret place
For me to smile.

1061

Snowflakes falling down
On my garden that once stood
Green in the summer.

1062

Twice this day I stood
Next to my barn and wished that
I could hear the storm.

1063

Fires in the night sky!
Call your makers and ask them
Why you're still shining.

1064

Embers of the fire
Glow softly in the darkness.
Never to return.

1065
The lonely leaves
Fall upon my garden now,
Waiting for winter.

1066
A picked peach eaten,
Leaves the pit for new peaches.
Plant your garden now!

1067
Rose petals landing
On the river's surfaces.
Along for the ride.

1068
The far mountain peaks
Point upward toward the
Moonlight and the drifting clouds.

1069
Over the valleys,
A calm wind blows silently,
Always going home.

1070
Bristles catch my legs,
Stop me in my tracks as I
Send my patience away.

1071
The puppies chased themselves
Around the garden fence,
While I waited there.

1072
While the puppets danced,
Grandfather watched his rice boil.
What say you old dog?

1073
Thick trees in my way,
I move around them into
The waters of the stream.

1074
Cornered in my barn,
The badger shows his sharp fangs.
But no forgiveness.

1075
Chasing kites in air,
Makes the sparrow seem dumber
Than he really is.

1076
The fog catches me,
And drags me along with it
Into the darkness.

1077
Centered in the sky,
The moon shines full and brighter
Than any one star.

1078
Ants follow my feet
Everywhere I go, even
When I stop for lunch.

1079
At the heart of it,
No one knows the answers to
All the reasons for.

1080
A jilted lover
Wonders at the sky at night.
Where did I go wrong?

1081
Falling on the sand,
The cinch bug turns himself over,
And dies then and there.

1082
The grass on the path
Reminds me of several
Wrestling matches.

1083
New baskets of rice
Taken to the village to cook.
Where will it end?

1084
Seven horsemen riding,
Finding their way along,
Looking for death.

1085
Chop down a dead tree,
And watch it grow several
New trees where it stood.

1086
Can you see where the
Mountain ends, and where the sky
Begins to blossom?

1087
A squirrel died here.
Yesterday afternoon.
Where does it all end?

1088
Tolerance is not
My best suit for knowing
What to do in life.

1089
Just enough space now
For all the eggs hatching.
The elm tree sadly cries.

1090
The earth swallows up
Everything that stands on it.
Never seen again!

1091
Up above the moon,
A monk suffers his penance.
For what I don't know.

1092
Gathering new shells,
The sand gives them up sadly.
The crabs do not care.

1093
A large fruit fly begs
For it knows not how to fetch
Its own evening meal.

1094
Small house in the mist,
Looking me over as I
Approach with a cat.

1095
Foolish crows crying,
Forgetting their lost minions,
Watching the goat laugh.

1096
Playing games of cards,
Watching the clouds form darkly,
A mountain restrains.

1097
A leaf floats along
The river's bank and dies there.
Does it mean something?

1098
Orphan sparrows
Spar with the afternoon wind,
Leaving me friendless.

1099
Homeless beetles with
Nowhere to go in the night
Except into bed.

1100
Where pearls lie fallow,
The sun dies shallow in mist.
All dragons gone now!

1101
Amusing squirrels
With convictions pocketed
My discoveries.

1102
Blighted acorns died,
Giving the ground below them
A new life and hope.

1103
A trickster in
Sheep's clothing has been following
Me around all day.

1104
The red colors of
Sunset abound in my mind.
Waiting another.

1105
Near the old mountains,
A long snake slithers along,
Coming this way.

1106
Across the new pond,
A vulture stands awaiting
To catch me alone.

1107

Spilling a bowl of rice,
I stand up and shout:
Come back into my dish!

1108

A long line of trees
Strings past my so lonely house,
Keeping me inside.

1109

The dust on my floor
Gathers in places so secret
I cannot find it.

1110

Cancel the concert!
The meadowlarks have decided
To sing us a song.

1111

Winter is on us.
Come back summer to warm us.
Why go away now?

1112

A beggar from town
Stole the fruit from my plum trees
For the wine he drinks.

1113

A single wood thrush
Stomped through the forest today.
Mad at the hornets.

1114
Trapped in my house,
A mouse struggles for freedom,
From what I don't know.

1115
Roses go to bed
Early at night, for the bees
Keep them company.

1116
In winter, the snows
Bury the grass in their depths
And with it their pasts.

1117
Carnations flower
Next to the path where I walk.
Keep away the deer.

1118
A lost butterfly
Can always find its way home
In the darkest night.

1119
Caterpillars wait
For just the right time of night
To express themselves.

1120
They can't hear me now.
Nor could they really ever.
For I am dead.

1121

How can a bluebird
Know ahead of time that I'm
Sowing my melons?

1122

Beyond horizons,
Someone tells someone else that
Winter is coming.

1123

Several people
Walking by my hut comment.
My window's open.

1124

Never before now
Could the harsh call of a dove
Be heard so loudly.

1125

Too fast! Too fast! Yells
A sparrow at me as I
Toss rice in the air.

1126

Under the low bridge,
A stooped-over raccoon lies
Hidden in waiting.

1127

A village so old
There's not one lonely house
Without a persimmon tree.

1128
Cast a large shadow,
For as the storm creeps upon
Us, it will not stop.

1129
A delicate rose
Hung in the balance between
A fence and forlorn.

1130
Buried in water, my rice took a
Hit from thunderous
Rain that kept coming.

1131
A wiry chipmunk,
Crouched beneath a half-buried
Log, whistling loud.

1132
Autumn's coolish hand
Paring away the land.
Eggplants, cucumbers!

1133
Having stood my ground,
The bear took a look over
His shoulder for help.

1134
Flower of the harvest moon.
It only looks that way
To a cotton field.

1135
Temptation leads far,
Too far for me to get to.
So that's the question.

1136
The monk peacefully drinks his
Morning tea while watching
Chrysanthemums bloom.

1137
Down beneath the earth
Stands a granite man so deep
That his voice is lost.

1138
The strongest of them
Took a look at me and smiled,
Then killed his foe fast.

1139
In my twilight years,
I notice the animals
Talking to me now.

1140
Chrysanthemum's scent.
In the garden, a worn out
Sandal. Just the sole.

1141
Kisos chestnuts for
A person of the floating
World. A souvenir!

1142
Banana plants in autumn.
Storm rain drips into tub,
Hearing the night.

1143
Halfway there I stopped
And gave my life a good look.
Nothing the hell here.

1144
A worm under
Moonlight secretly crawls into
A chestnut at night.

1145
Could someone now be
Knocking at my door seeking
Food or something else?

1146
Higher than a skylark,
Resting in the sky
On a mountain pass.

1147
A sickly duck,
Falling down in the dark cold,
To sleep overnight.

1148
After awhile,
Even though sad,
Cormorant fishing again.

1149

Without turning into
A butterfly, autumn strengthens
For the worm.

1150

I'm tired of kids.
For the person who says this,
There are no flowers.

1151

In the world outside,
Is it harvesting time?
The grass near my hut.

1152

From this very day,
Erase the inscription in dew
On the bamboo hat.

1153

Death comes softly for
Those who seek repose in it.
But it's forever.

1154

Walking on and on,
Even through I fall down tired
In fields of clover.

1155

Whispers loudly say,
That a storm's on its way back,
Having driven past.

1156

Lost battles survive
In the forests around us.
We remember them.

1157

Could the fireflies stop
Showing off their bright candles?
A mouse said to me.

1158

Along the way somewhere
I met a strange old farmer
Wandering his fields.

1159

Standing upon its
Uppermost branches, a wren
Captures wind in its wings.

1160

Too few thunderclouds
To bring us a torrential
Rain for tonight.

1161

So many forests,
Giving me so little time
To wander in them.

1162

Thin from its Kiso trip,
And still not yet recovered,
The late harvest moon.

1163

Buying a measure box,
I now feel differently about
Moon viewing.

1164

Viewing the moon,
No one at my party
Has such a beautiful face.

1165

Out of the blue sky
Comes a bedeviled falcon,
Aiming right at me.

1166

The full moon. Seven
Songs of a woman turning
Towards the sea.

1167

The uppermost branch
Of a big oak tree standing
Has nothing to hide.

1168

Sleeping in the temple,
The serious looking face
Is viewing the moon.

1169

A seed-sized beetle
Sneaks a peak from underground
At me disappearing.

1170
The moon so pure,
A wandering monk carries it
Across the sand.

1171
Icicles dancing
On a straight line in the snow.
My clothes dancing, too.

1172
I caught a rainbow
From the lake in the morning,
And ate it for lunch.

1173
Calling out his name,
The dog came running again,
Finding me at home.

1174
Quietly robbing
Eggs from a nest, the lonely
Cuckoo does his job.

1175
On top of mountains
Comes a dark cloud sailing by,
Catching the top peak.

1176
In the deep dark woods,
Several animals group
To make their new plans.

1177

A slimy green worm
Stretches out before my eyes,
Wasting no time.

1178

Down deep in lilies
A frog tries to leap safely
To the sands of shore.

1179

Dazzling sunlight
Reflects off my window bright.
Leaving me alone.

1180

The rank odor of
Death catches me by surprise
And colors him dead.

1181

Flocks of robins
Flew by my hut after noon,
Wasting no time there.

1182

Riding in my cart
On the way to the village,
I come upon death.

1183

All my hates and loves
Did little good against their
Machinery of death.

1184
The afternoon sunlight
Shines in that way it can when
Memories seduce.

1185
A kite flying high
Gave me wonder that being
Tied to me is good.

1186
The blue of the sea
Against the gray of the fog
And now only me.

1187
Where does it all go,
After so many years and years
All gone in a flash?

1188
A pony gets born
And stands up for the first time,
Looking in my eyes.

1189
Too few fathers
Take the time to foster their
Children's caresses.

1190
Digging deep under,
I found a beautiful coin
That someone left here.

1191
Rapidly dying,
A fly lays trembling in my
Cup of warm cider.

1192
From times long ago,
I remember the soft touch
Of a mother's hand.

1193
Warm spring butterflies
Flittering this way and that.
Whither do you go?

1194
The smoke from my fire
Goes up through my chimney tall.
Out into the night.

1195
Walking backwards now,
I cannot help but think that
Many do not think.

1196
Awake before dawn,
I slip into my kitchen
And pour a cup of tea.

1197
In the blink of an
Eye, a meteor blazed in
The sky above me.

1198
Everywhere I look,
I can see the tenderness
Of angry robins.

1199
Warm spring evening,
Give me your tender loving
Songs of beauty.

1200
Across the table
I saw my mother standing.
Cautioning me still.

1201
Stories follow me
As I travel towards the sea,
Finally dying.

1202
The flavorful smell
Of heat cooking wildflowers,
Made my tea tasty.

1203
Up above the trees,
The wrens fly in circles,
Waiting for the sun to set.

1204
The river flows down
Toward the shores of the sea,
Hoping to catch a salmon.

1205
Underneath the lake
Lies a clam worth digging up
And adding to rice.

1206
Canyon's chasms hold
Forests, trees, lakes, meadows,
Streams, cloudy listless thoughts.

1207
She who is no more
Must have left fine clothes that
Now need summer airing.

1208
Shallows at Shiogoshi.
Cool and wide cranes hop
And ponder in the tide.

1209
This windswept field
Of summer grass. All that's left
Of valorous deeds. Alas.

1210
A shady willow
By a stump I stop to rest.
I'm stopping still.

1211
Grab hold of the night,
Give it a good shaking,
Make it behave itself.

1212

High above the stars,
A comet begins its tail,
Stretching for the moon.

1213

As the sun sets,
So does the night come around,
Catching us off guard.

1214

Sandpipers digging,
Hoping to catch a taste of
Sand crab underneath.

1215

The fire bristles with
Sparks that fly in the night sky,
Waking the green frogs.

1216

Toward a distant isle,
The cuckoo flies, fading in the
Mist its forlorn cries.

1217

Mountain spirit,
I discern your face in the blazing
Blossoms of this place.

1218

You prepare the fire,
Tea, and bowl, whilst I, a giant
Snowball, go and roll.

1219
A cautious small grin
Gave me a similar grin
In return from her.

1220
High above the heath,
A skylark sings unattached
To any earthly things.

1221
A black bear enters
The river mouth above me,
Catching his day's fish.

1222
Silly meadowlarks
Sit in the grass waiting for
Darkness to arrive.

1223
A bear caught me tight
In its big bear's stifling grip.
Hugging me to death.

1224
On top of mountains,
Clouds cluster around glaciers
Waiting for the thunder.

1225
Fallow fields of rice
Stand ready for the planting.
And so do the birds.

1226

The gull in his nest
Studies the horizon for
Whatever comes next.

1227

Terraced fields of rice
Climb up the mountain above.
The room where I sleep.

1228

Could it be tonight,
That a pair of comets meet
And turn into one?

1229

A single moonbeam
Turns into many when it
Reflects from water.

1230

Along the small trail
I spot a small doe sniffing
As for its mother.

1231

Spring is here and a
Morning haze hovers above
That nameless hill.

1232

The same old oak. Am I
Useless aloof? Hail pounding
On a brand new roof.

1233
His wife sculpted a
Vase and discovered winter
In its dirty corpse.

1234
A winter's night.
The sound of an oar makes me weep.
Chills me to the core.

1235
The wind is brisk,
The hour late, dead leaves swirl
Against my flimsy gate.

1236
I throw a small rock,
And it skips across water
Into a wasps' nest.

1237
Mister spider, you don't sing much.
The autumn wind in whose
Sigh you sway.

1238
Bobbing on the waves,
Sipping wine, and gazing tipsy
At the moon divine.

1239
A high in the sky sun
Beats down on my head of hair
And teaches wonder.

1240
Among these summer trees,
A pasania.
Something to count on.

1241
A sliver of moon
Crests the winter horizon
And leaves me breathless.

1242
The snake below me,
Tells me of his woes and fears,
Calls for the black bear.

1243
I see the moon sail
Slowly above the mountain.
Whither go you now?

1244
Leaves of green color
Fall to the ground around me
Now that I am blind.

1245
A trail of red blood
Follows me everywhere now.
Why am I bleeding?

1246
Sadness prevails now
Because the Buddha has left
For his summer home.

1247

I cannot see you
Anymore. Things have gone Wrong with what they should
be.

1248

The music in my
Eyes, mouth, nose, soul, and ears
Has taken my breath away.

1249

Cannot we stop it?
Changing the rules as we go?
Falling behind our trust?

1250

Over the mountains,
Away toward the sea, beyond
I cannot believe.

1251

Cedar umbrellas
Off to Mount Yoshimo for
The cherry blossoms.

1252

On my way to town,
A stranger meets me, speaking
Of the parades there.

1253

Catching a few winks,
I lie in the back of my
Wagon in the field.

1254
Can you believe the
Stories that my grandmother
Tells about me?

1255
Waters dip lower,
When the fall comes closer
To the day of days.

1256
A cautious robin
Flies low from the horizon
Over my garden.

1257
Once again flowers
Point toward the sunlight's
Wonder and speak of their lives.

1258
A spider celebrates
Another day of webbing.
And a fly's death.

1259
Clouds and thunderstorms
Cover the sky around me
And my garden's thirst.

1260
Frogs dancing in light.
Celebrating the onset
Of spring's awakening.

1261

Death comes knocking
At my door tonight unwelcome.
Nonetheless it comes.

1262

Over the next hill
Stands a scarecrow scaring crows
Away from gardens.

1263

Tall pine trees surround
A small meadow of grasses.
The sunlight sleeps here.

1264

Tongue-tied red tail hawks
Gathered together over
The meadow's dung pile.

1265

Along the river,
Several frogs gather
Together to wrestle.

1266

Pissing in a field,
My neighbor saw a black bear
Watching him there.

1267

Dark and lonely nights
Maintained their dreams of
Sorrow and my yesterdays.

1268
Come little robins,
Into my arms for a hug.
That's what the deer says.

1269
The fog comes early,
Blocking the sunlight from my
Garden's better half.

1270
Counting the bushes,
I miss one or two and
Begin counting again.

1271
Clever little wrens,
Cooling off in their hollows.
Where did the bear go?

1272
All the day long,
Yet not long enough for the
Skylark. Singing! Singing!

1273
My father died then,
Just after he'd gone asleep
That night long ago.

1274
The sparrows take baths
When the puddles surround them,
And dry when they don't.

1275

Happiness abounds
Where wood thrushes thrush
Around, in between gardens.

1276

A tremendous storm
Exploded in the night sky,
Leaving me breathless.

1277

Worms crawl in the mud
Escaping the dreaded wrens
That eat them for lunch.

1278

The bark on the tree
Protects it from the gremlins.
And, of course, from me.

1279

Wriggling fish I hooked,
Struggling to gain its freedom.
Winning it at last!

1280

Slipping into robes,
I stand alone in the dark
Waiting for the dawn.

1281

Monstrous green slime
Crawls out from the lake toward me.
Why does it do that?

1282
Dead daffodils lay
All about me as I walk
Toward infinity.

1283
Boats line the harbor
Waiting for their masters to
Drag them out to sea.

1284
Bounty from the sea.
The dead fish line my table
Giving me their meat.

1285
The colorful light
Comes from the highest of skies,
Leaving me behind.

1286
My sandals get wet.
But slipping into their cords
Makes me sad again.

1287
Along the seashore
Walks a crab sideways until
No more sand exists.

1288
Outside and above
There sits a big black raven
Waiting for my dog.

1289
Lying in bed now,
I think of two ideas.
Rice and my green tea.

1290
Imagining hilltops
Basking in the summer sun,
With me on my back.

1291
Noble watercress.
Why do you wander over
Near where the frogs go?

1292
I found a rat's nest
Sitting in my garden right
Where it shouldn't be.

1293
Spitting words at me,
Chickadees run in circles.
Great black bears in caves.

1294
Wandering kitten.
Where do you think your going?
Why do you want that?

1295
A night without rain.
A day without sunshine.
Can winter be far behind?

1296
Sadness takes its toll
When the weather brings back
The winter snowfall.

1297
Wrinkled old men stand
Like statues near a river
Waiting their turns.

1298
Cicadas buzzing
Through the night and day
Humming tunes that elude me.

1299
Every gust of wind
Changes the butterfly's place
On the oak tree.

1300
Calligraphers use
Pens and inks to draw pictures
Of one thousand words.

1301
Canaries sing songs
Of quite lengthy invention.
My children sing, too!

1302
The mosquitos bite deep
Into my arms and legs.
Slapping does little good.

1303
High in the mountains,
A deer wanders lost and sad,
Waiting its mother's help.

1304
A canal brings water
For me and my garden dry,
Feeding the hard soil.

1305
Delicious green apples
High above me on branches
Dropping now like flies.

1306
Dreaming in my bed,
Of cherries bright and red,
Has brought me here today.

1307
Finding mother is
A wonderful thing to see.
Even in death.

1308
A pond lies still
In the meadow across the way.
Waiting for the lost.

1309
The sun through the clouds
Gives me the fullest story
Of all of my life.

1310
The windy orchard
Brings along a cold winter
And an icy snow.

1311
Over tea my brother
Reminds me of his lost dog.
And of why he came.

1312
Give me the basis
Of a story worth telling,
Says my grandfather.

1313
A skeleton of man
Stands at my door waiting for
The rest of the story.

1314
Fear begets tensions,
Confidence overrides fear,
And love begets fear.

1315
Buddha waits for me
Standing in the courtyard still,
As I come too late.

1316
How can a simple
Man keep going in this world
When all is not well?

1317
Berries often make
The very best pies to eat
Along with my tea.

1318
A sliver of moon
Catches the frog as he jumps.
Marking him for death.

1319
Fearless hornets die.
Jumping to conclusions,
Stinging the scarecrow.

1320
Empty are my bowls
Of rice and tea for me.
The garden rests now.

1321
Twenty-seven blackbirds,
Sitting on my fencepost,
Looking at the ground.

1322
The tallest branches
Stay well above the snows,
But hang with icicles.

1323
In the last light of
Day, the mouse seeks refuge in
My everlasting soul.

1324
Along a swift creek,
A lone man waits forever
For his wife to return.

1325
Music never stops.
It only pretends to so
We can ponder it.

1326
Could a great spider
Cause the earth to shudder hard?
Or was that a quake?

1327
A sloppy berry
Makes for a tiring snack
As I try to eat it.

1328
Circles cannot do,
For once they begin they can
Never come to an end.

1329
A sudden bright flash
Causes me to look for a cause.
A storm coming!

1330
Red sunsets follow
A long day of hard work,
Bringing the night along.

1331

Dancing meadowlarks,
Sitting in the trees watching
The cows eating grass.

1332

A wagon comes by.
A storm follows in the sky.
Why does it not know?

1333

Water drips the rain down
From my windowsill giving
Me no peace at all.

1334

Cold ice on rivers,
Floating downstream as with
Boats carrying monkeys.

1335

In a cast iron
Barrel, a mother rat sits,
Her babies suckling.

1336

A bird in the sky
Flies around forever it
Seems, never knowing.

1337

The owl loves to sit,
Waiting to strike its victim
When the time is right.

1338
Nightfall bends the wind.
Darkness, evil, hollow moons,
Never, ever end.

1339
Shining on my roof,
A lost metal bracelet
Belonging to me.

1340
Cannot the fervor
Over the river's ending
Be postponed to now?

1341
Water snakes writhe,
Water splashes in their wake,
A frog heads for home.

1342
The fire crackles loud
In the morning air as I
Wander on the path.

1343
Clouds will separate
The two friends after migrating.
Wild geese departing.

1344
Sleeping under stars,
Brings the bears out from hiding,
And me to my hut.

1345
From all directions,
Winds bring petals of cherries
Into the grebe lake.

1346
Summer zashiki.
Make more and enter the
Mountain and the garden.

1347
The reeds in the lake
Move in the windy morning,
Waiting for noon storms.

1348
When summer's rain comes,
Filling the lakes with water
And refreshing me.

1349
A brisk cup of tea,
Makes thinking wiser than me,
Or so it would seem.

1350
I cannot see fog,
For the cloudy air keeps me
From finding it there.

1351
Water from the skies
Leaks down upon my hut and
Leaves me breathlessly.

1352
A tolerant man
Reflects on his natural stance
Against all lost fruits.

1353
Along my way home
A meadow stops me and asks
What is my hurry?

1354
To the leg of a heron,
Adding a long shank
Of a pheasant.

1355
Too few of my friends
Believe in ghosts for me to
Make them understand.

1356
The tree above me
Gasps for air as the summer's
Heat grips it in hand.

1357
On high narrow road, an old
Traveler clears a wide swath,
Tiny scythe glinting.

1358
See surviving sons
Visit the ancestral graves,
Bearded with bent canes.

1359
If there were fragrance,
These heavy snowflakes settling
Lilies on the rocks.

1360
This snowy morning,
That black crow I hate so much.
But he's beautiful!

1361
No oil to read by,
I am off to bed, but ah,
My moonlit pillow.

1362
Across the meadow
And up onto the mountain,
The searchers wandered.

1363
Cold first winter rain.
Poor monkey, you too could use
A little woven cape.

1364
First white snow of fall,
Just enough to bend the leaves
From faded daffodils.

1365
At every land's end,
The water holds a special
Place in all our hearts.

1366
Dry cheerful cricket,
Chirping keeps the autumn gay,
Contemptuous of frost.

1367
Cast aside your food,
For no one may eat this day.
Buddha has spoken!

1368
The doe shook his fur,
Walked into the stable grace,
And stood there smiling.

1369
The look on his face
Gave me wonder that he could
Look me in the eyes.

1370
Now in sad autumn,
As I take my darkening path,
A lonely bird.

1371
Will we meet again?
Here at your flowering grave,
Two white butterflies.

1372
Hidden are the groves
Of plum trees in the willows,
That only brave ones go.

1373
Calligraphers draw
On paper so thin that it
Cowers before them.

1374
Silver shines the moon.
Full as its circle allows,
Ready to explode.

1375
Nine times arising,
To see the moon, whose solemn
Pace marks only midnight yet.

1376
Down the road he comes,
Bearing gifts of many men,
Waiting for his coins.

1377
Comes a horse's knight,
Fighting the battles that fright
Even the best men.

1378
The sea darkening.
Oh voices of the wild ducks,
Crying, whirling white.

1379
Below the waterfall,
The fish swim fast and lively,
Blowing bubbles there.

1380
Comes a love so strong,
That everything's forgotten
Except its calling.

1381
Hush goes the moonlight,
Threatening to fall from the sky,
If I do not comply.

1382
Now the bridge swinging
Has quieted the snakes,
Like our entwined life.

1383
In the twilight rains,
The brilliant hued hibiscus.
A lovely sunset.

1384
Crescent moon above.
Tell me the stories I want
To hear fore I die.

1385
Too few of the nights
That surround my bed, give me
Dreams that I like.

1386
In the summer's breeze
Comes the last of the crickets
Calling for its mate.

1387

Long ago, on dark nights
I saw the moon shimmer,
Where you are standing.

1388

Tender are the plums
That fall so quietly now
That I cannot hear.

1389

Glowing in the night,
My fire brings me silently
To the edge of sleep.

1390

Across my kitchen,
Comes the rancor of my cat
Chasing a big rat.

1391

Silly little bugs,
Shouting profanities towards
Other little bugs.

1392

Too few bees flying
To gather the flower's strength
To make their honey.

1393

Up above and high
Come the eagle's flight towards me,
Gathering anger.

1394
Lost are my lonely
Days of silence, when the doves
Tiptoed through my life.

1395
Towards the horizon,
A flame shoots forward and up.
The dawn is nearing.

1396
A spinster's hopeless
Search for something that cannot
Be, comes to me.

1397
Comes a spider crawling,
Chasing a dying beetle
Round my table.

1398
Sacks of only rice,
Spring leaks on my only floor
Of my only hut.

1399
The enduring light
That shatters my only hope
That dawn will begin.

1400
A bear comes running,
Seeking his lunch from my sack
Of pears on my back.

1401
The road ahead takes
Many turns and many hills.
So much still to see.

1402
Undercover of
Night, the owl selects targets,
And makes good on them.

1403
Behind my garden,
Several gophers plot their
Future plans for it.

1404
In the height of fate,
No one escapes whatever
Makes them what they are.

1405
Pine needle droppings
Litter the forest floor here,
Making me wear shoes.

1406
In the blink of eye,
Two possible outcomes as
One, the vulture says.

1407
Several anthills
Stand in a row like soldiers
Waiting for warfare.

1408
Foraging in trees,
A muskrat discovers a
Termite mound alone.

1409
Trees that stand above,
Brave the seasons with sorrow,
But never regret.

1410
A section of mountain
Fell down in an avalanche
Rocking my old hut.

1411
Soon the winter comes,
Bathing us all in cold snow.
We can't avoid it.

1412
There stood a blackbird,
Staring at me with black eyes,
Wondering aloud.

1413
Silent the old town.
The scent of flowers floating
And evening bells.

1414
Wake! The sky is light.
Let us to the road again,
Companion butterfly.

1415
Old dark sleepy pool,
Quick unsuspecting frog
Goes plop. Waters splash!

1416
Swallow in the dusk,
Spare my little buzzing friends
Among the flowers.

1417
Intense summer winds
Can give me the creeps alone,
For they never stop.

1418
Must springtime fade?
Then cry all birds and cold fishes,
Pale eyes pour tears.

1419
Something standing there,
In the dark shadows of my
Kitchen. A sparrow.

1420
A moonbeam rises
Until it reaches the mountain.
And there it shines bright.

1421
Waves come roaring in.
The battered shoreline stands
Firm. Nature fights nature.

1422
My back to the wind,
The sail in front of my eyes,
Come what may, my God.

1423
A long line of bears
Standing together where none
Would have stood before.

1424
Resting from walking,
A lone man struggles to stand,
Wishing himself home.

1425
A morning bell sounds,
Waking me from deepest sleep,
Welcoming again.

1426
Temples stand erect
For many years beyond them,
To remind us.

1427
A pocket of coins
Makes me eager to get lost.
Somewhere to spend them.

1428
A bush full of wrens
Jumps to life as I pass by.
Scaring me to death.

1429
A long way from home,
I stop to rest a minute.
Wishing for times end.

1430
Living in the forest
Aside my fire at night.
Too many sounds come round.

1431
The smallest of bugs,
Skittering around my house,
Wishing I would go.

1432
Clever boys and girls,
Can make mothers and fathers
Crazy for their souls.

1433
Who can tell me this?
When an eagle leaves the ground,
Why does he then miss?

1434
I caught a large mouse,
Running through my garden plot,
Leaving me no choice.

1435
A bat flew over
My head last night and worried
Me almost to death.

1436
Fishing the river,
I caught a cold, not a fish.
Why did that happen?

1437
Nearer to a God,
The black bear looked up at me,
And smiled ear to ear.

1438
Clouds of cherry blooms,
Tolling twilight bells,
Temple light the night.

1439
Too curious flower,
Watching us pass, met death.
Our hungry donkey.

1440
Under cherry trees. Soup,
A salad, fish, and all
Seasoned with petals.

1441
Next to a fence post
Sat a rabbit looking at me.
Waiting for what?

1442
Under the ground here,
I found a chestnut buried,
And I gave it back.

1443

The window looks right
At me in many strange ways.
Say hello to it!

1444

Back at my door now,
I stand facing the mountain,
Looking up at God.

1445

In the middle of
Life comes a wild winter's time,
When nothing comes back.

1446

Crossover the road,
Get to the garden, and turn.
There you will find it.

1447

The life of a saint
Cannot be compared with mine,
For mine thinks of me.

1448

Up the mountain crest,
Past glaciers and rivers both,
A large antelope.

1449

Across the lake from here,
A wounded bear lips his leg,
And waits for winter.

1450
Down the road apiece,
An old man spits in his yard
And counts his pigeons.

1451
The beauties of the
Heavy worn earth gave salvation
To my enemies.

1452
There's always something
That goes astray when you know
What happens to you.

1453
A starving mouse needs
Food to survive the winter.
But then the eagles.

1454
How can I blossom,
When so many are trying
To blossom, too?

1455
Cancel the show now,
For the actors decided
To call it a night.

1456
The drama of life
Plays itself out over time.
But not over me.

1457
In the early dawn,
Feathers fall from the trees as
Birds pruning be.

1458
The lights of the town
Keep me awake in the night,
Lying in bed like that.

1459
Color my cheeks red,
And give me the coins of life.
For never I came.

1460
Who says the night owl
And I know not who be,
Since ever I was?

1461
In the darkest night,
Two eyes follow me in fright,
Of me and of them.

1462
Down by the seashore,
An old woman builds nests of
Straw, and birds come flying.

1463
In every deep pot,
A small creature grows larger,
Making my day long.

1464
Along came a man,
Singing to everyone loud,
Asking for money.

1465
Bees make honey
In hives by the river wall.
Right next to my hut.

1466
Eagles soar above
Waiting for nothing to be
But what it is now.

1467
The hummingbird sings
With its wings lulling me to sleep,
And him to eat.

1468
In a certain way,
The world sees a robin much
As a robin the world.

1469
The heat of mid-day
Brings about far reaching,
But noble thoughts.

1470
Glorious the moon.
Therefore our thanks to dark
Clouds, come to rest our necks.

1471
Dewdrops let me cleanse
In your briefsweet waters
These dark hands of life.

1472
Who can tell a wren
What time of day it is,
Or when he should die?

1473
A roadrunner sings
In the happiest of ways
As he breezes by.

1474
Grief strikes home when the
Winter comes with a big bang
Instead of a whimper.

1475
Brothers and sisters
Have too many problems,
And too many sorrows.

1476
The breaks that we make,
Take too long to transpire now,
So I regret them.

1477
An egret stands alone
On the back of a cow,
Waiting for something.

1478
Why so scrawny a cat
Starving for fat fish or mice?
Or backyard love?

1479
Seas are wild tonight.
Stretching over Sado Island,
Silent clouds of stars.

1480
Ah me! I am the one
Who spends his little breakfast
Morning glory gazing.

1481
A cave that I know
Goes deeper than you can go.
Deeper even more.

1482
Can you believe me,
That the colors of rainbows
Begin with the sky?

1483
Curvatures in air,
Make it seem to me that bears
Never cross the line.

1484
The origins of time,
Begin with the birth of bears,
For they own the world.

1485
Light shines here upon
The dark shadows of my life,
Waiting for me.

1486
Comes a silent snake,
Readying to strike at will.
Stand back everyone!

1487
A lone mosquito
At night is a true nightmare.
Awake in my bed.

1488
Flies buzz around me,
Waiting for the right time,
To dive bomb my head.

1489
In shallow water,
A spider weaves part of its web,
Waiting for fish.

1490
A grouse hunts for food.
Never happy or sad, but
Hungry all the same.

1491
Snakes silently crawl
Around on the ground below,
Wasting not their time.

1492
A nest in the trees
High up above me in air,
Catching a silent wind.

1493
Seeking a black bear.
I found him sitting in water
Taking a long bath.

1494
My fence falling down,
Fell on the fence that fell down,
Before it fell down.

1495
In my sock go coins,
Waiting for the time I go
Shopping with my dog.

1496
Seven times seven,
Says the robin to the wren.
Too many numbers.

1497
Around the slick stones,
Sitting in the lake waters,
Ready for stepping on.

1498
A brown beaver swims
Toward me this morning, singing
His tune of good day.

1499
As far as the sky
From where I now stand alone
Waiting for you.

1500
In the canyon deep,
A forest and a lake keep
Me and my dog safe.

1501
Comes a monstrous
Black bear toward my house
Today. Run says the dormouse!

1502
The knob on my door
Turned to the left, and then
To the right. No sound!

1503
A rainbow curves
Over the distant mountains,
Begging me to come.

1504
Stars wink in the sky,
Seducing me into coming
Their way tonight.

1505
Mountain rose petals
Falling, falling, falling now.
Waterfall music.

1506
Twilight whippoorwills
Whistle of sweet, deep innocence,
Dark loneliness.

1507
Lightning starts a fire,
And then along comes rain
And puts the fire out.

1508
A soft petal lands
Near to my heart, but spares me
Its forlorn story.

1509
An urn by my door
Is filled with the waters of
Winter's long journey.

1510
A tear in my eye,
Shows all of my sorrows.
My father is dead.

1511
When waters grow cold,
The snow is not far behind.
And then winter arrives.

1512
The braggart begins
To tell his stories to me.
The later it gets!

1513
Comes a whippoorwill
Onto my kitchen sill, waiting
For I know not what.

1514
Several bluebirds
Cackle away at the nests,
Where robins' eggs grow.

1515
Her problems gave the
Heavily weathered donkey
A bigger burden.

1516
Icicles hang low
From above my door and roof,
Dripping days away.

1517
Too few meadowlarks
To go around, now that the
Winds begin to blow.

1518
Music can be found
In nature's mountains and glens.
Never to be lost.

1519
Sad is an old man
Who lives his life without love.
For he knows nothing.

1520
Give it to heaven,
And heaven will give it back,
But in different ways.

1521
Carry a long bed
Onto the meadow floor,
And I'll sleep one more day.

1522
Sorrows lend me ears!
For no sorrow have I,
That I have not left behind.

1523
A bowl of hot rice
And a cup of hotter tea.
Breakfast comes at last.

1524
Send me your paupers.
Give them a meal and a bed,
And I'll do the rest.

1525
A wiry old fox,
Destined to die very soon,
Runs along the shore.

1526
A long way away,
A crystal goblet vibrates
In the winter's wind.

1527
Dust motes in the sun
Dance in the light below
My open window.

1528
A whirlwind circles,
Waiting for the right time to
Collect its reward.

1529
Down towards the blue lake,
A warren criticizes
My choice of clothing.

1530
A rug and a rag
Lie on the floor of my hut,
Acting their best roles.

1531
An old cedar tree
Down by the bridge across waters
Keeping its watch.

1532
Wind chimes chime at once,
For the wind softly blows now,
Waiting for music.

1533
Waves on the sea's shore
Stand up straight towards the sky,
When there's a big storm.

1534
Five birds on a wire,
Talking to no one, not even
Themselves. What next?

1535
On top of a ridge,
A lone eagle sits idly,
Watching the moon set.

1536
The mountains grow cold,
And the animals come down,
To wait until spring.

1537
Comes a dark stranger.
Walking along on the path
Toward the meadow.

1538
In the dead of night,
I took a walk by the lake
And saw a firefly.

1539
A cup of green tea
Gives me a sense of order
When none otherwise.

1540
In the sea's surf
Edge mingling with bright
Small shells, soft clover petals.

1541
White cloud of mist,
Above white cherry blossoms,
Dawn shining mountain.

1542
Ballet in the air.
Twin butterflies become one
When they mate.

1543
Black cloudbank broken,
Scatters in the night. Now see
Moonlighted mountains.

1544
Curiously a cat
Crawls upon a cantaloupe
And stares into space.

1545
A cautious butterfly
Flies into the wind as it
Chases down the night.

1546
Yesterday's nightmare
Can become today's journey.
Welcome to Monday.

1547
Stand against the night,
For all the good it will do.
For night must fall.

1548
Dead leaves in the fall,
Shiver in the cool air,
And sail in the wind.

1549
Winds so strong blowing,
That the tree limbs touch the
Ground, bending not breaking.

1550
The old man quivers
Under the moon. Chilly night.
Trying to stay warm.

1551
At the top of a hill
A nameless bird stands blithely
Forgetting itself.

1552
Comes the deadly night,
Hiding all manner of fright,
And no one comes out.

1553
In the deep puddles,
Worms wriggle around trying
Not to drown themselves.

1554
Next to my front gate
Stands no one at all but a
Lost goat bleating loud.

1555
The plight of robins
Depends on a moment's dare,
For eagles fly high.

1556
Blowfish puff their cheeks
Into the water beyond.
Nothing but hot air.

1557
Comes the wind a roar.
Pushing a tide of snowflakes
Back into the storm.

1558
On the canyon walls,
Seagulls build their nests up high,
Waiting for the tide's fall.

1559
Creatures big and small
Come to me in bunches now.
Where is the black bear?

1560
As the fog moves out,
The clouds come in and cover
All of our daylight.

1561
Of the fifteen wrens
Standing on a laundry line,
Which one will go first?

1562
History of flies
Gives one a sense that past things
Have useless meanings.

1563
He took his sour mood
And deposited it with the bear
Who gave it to me.

1564
Crushing shells softly
Underfoot as he walks by,
Not noticing them.

1565
On a fresh spring day,
My rice lies sleeping in fields,
Waiting for the night.

1566
April's air stirs in
Willow leaves. A butterfly
Floats and balances.

1567
Out of the shadows,
An eagle soars high above,
Wings flying slowly.

1568
Curtains on windows,
Blowing softly in the wind,
Calling me to them.

1569
A muddy turtle
Climbs upon a winter limb
Hoping for a ride.

1570
Across the pacific,
A boat drifts this way and that,
Hoping to find me.

1571
When does the comet
Fly across the sky at night?
Comes the seldom seen!

1572
A fence stands between
Me and my neighbor's garden.
Stormy weather now.

1573
Finding its mother,
A happy wood thrush grabs her,
And loves her the more.

1574
Towering above,
The bells of the temple tall,
Ringing my health back.

1575
Severed heads abound
On the table near by bed.
Come not hornets here!

1576
Into the heavens
Go the souls of the many
Who stand for many.

1577
The bells have rung twice
For the sake of my father
Whose soul rises now.

1578
For viewing the moon,
Gather your strangers quite soon,
To see the old man.

1579
Beetles come around
Whenever there is food here.
Be gone scavengers.

1580
My stomach has fits
When the trout avoid my line,
And leave me hungry.

1581
Smiling, she quiets
All that she sees around her,
With nothing to lose.

1582
Symmetry abounds,
When water meets the shoreline,
To lead me toward home.

1583
Along the way to town,
I met a man that claims
Not to be following me.

1584
A cup of dark tea
In the morning with my rice,
Makes everything fine.

1585
Firecrackers behold!
The sky explodes with their lights.
New Year comes again.

1586
A snail slithers by,
Whistling as it goes, cautious
For an errant slime.

1587
When the stars were born,
The mountains saw them first,
And tallied up the score.

1588
Japanese poets
Have a way with words. Indeed,
So few for so much.

1589
Bears are everywhere.
Up on my roof, standing still,
Scaring me to death.

1590
Cast an iron hand
Over the beast from afar.
It comes not for you!

1591
In the morning sky,
Two falcons fly over my
Seldom used eye.

1592
How to catch a snake
As it whips around in grass.
Grab handfuls of squirm.

1593
Fanciful ducklings
Wander about my garden,
Wondering out loud.

1594
Curious dogs go on
Sniffing the garbage today,
Licking their lips.

1595
Fanciful fancies,
My house for a duckling's quack,
My love for its beak.

1596
Now that eyes of hawks
In dusky nightare darkened,
Chirping of the quails.

1597
A moth towards a flame
Makes me wish that I could save
Its life again.

1598
Fireflies tempt me
To garner their love and trust,
As I watch them burn.

1599
A house sits alone,
Guarding the forest from those
Who would burn it down

1600
Tall hedgerows of ducks
Surround my garden to keep
Me from going in.

1601
The walls of my hut
Catch all of the sounds and smells
That begin right here.

1602
Let the monkey dance.
She told me after I had
Asked him to stop.

1603
The lives of many
Come not to provide sorrow,
But to give solace.

1604
Fanciful fancies,
My house for a duckling's quack,
My love for your kiss.

1605
Up ahead, a house.
Waiting no doubt for the snow
Coming behind me.

1606
My soul discovers
The soft music in my heart,
Asking me to die.

1607
I am the music
That comes from everywhere here,
And never leaving.

1608
My grandfather told
The very best of stories
To me and my dog.

1609
I hear music
Wafting in from the meadows
Singing to me.

1610
Windows in my hut
Shake in the howling winter.
Winds outside!

1611

A dusty muskrat
Shakes itself loose from the dirt
And gives me a glare.

1612

Snow rises above
The top of my door and traps me
Inside of my hut.

1613

Repeating all this
For everyone to hear
The anger in my voice.

1614

Clouds betray themselves
As their shadows march across
The meadow swamps.

1615

For a lovely bowl,
Let us arrange these flowers,
Since there is no rice.

1616

Ominous warnings!
The winter comes alone now,
Not waiting for me.

1617

A wicked snowstorm
Blew into my room catching
My yesterday's cold.

1618
Suddenly summer!
From a brief shower to a
Long rainstorm it comes.

1619
Catching a badger,
Fighting for its life again,
Having not found it.

1620
A long trestle bridge
Spans the river covering
A school of pupfish.

1621
A soliloquy
Of anger caught my mindless
Self, speaking out loud.

1622
The brilliance of night.
Clouds blanket the stars above
Leaving me breathless.

1623
The grass had grown tall,
Thinking it had never grown
In the field at all.

1624
The summer's ending,
So now we must put apart
Our last differences.

1625
A void of gladness
Sought its home in me today.
Granting me sadness.

1626
A long way away,
A war wages itself now,
Hopefully over.

1627
A caress of light
Woke me this morning again,
Leaving me alone.

1628
Very tall trees stood
Waiting for a good wind to
Blow them down again.

1629
Cabbage stew for lunch,
Along with a cup of tea.
My life in a rut.

1630
Rivers falls down falls
Gathering all the blowfish,
Rainbows, and lightning.

1631
Two sweet old ladies,
Struggled along the pathway
Leading to a lake.

1632
The road to nowhere.
Filled with people I've never
Known, following me home.

1633
Out from the darkness
Came a light as bright as the sun,
Scaring me to death.

1634
Out from its deep hole,
The head of a gopher peeks,
Looking me over.

1635
Suddenly rainstorms
Gave me a start, and a certain
Feeling of anger.

1636
Chasing each other,
A chipmunk and a badger
Take no prisoners.

1637
Seven bright rainbows
Caught today as I walked home
After fishing.

1638
A house full of dreams,
Empty now for the no one's
Home anymore.

1639
The trees give their leaves.
The limbs point their barren tips
Toward the stars above.

1640
The fall of the year
Makes everyone's sadness come.
Can't wait for winter.

1641
Silly little grouse,
Why do you constantly pout?
Can't you be alone?

1642
Spring around the bend,
Coming toward me like a bus,
Waiting for no one.

1643
A dry dusty world
Peeks out from my garden's thirst
And swallows my mind.

1644
Calling to its mate,
A whippoorwill sounds so sad
I want to help him.

1645
His stock and trade gone,
The farmer takes his shovel
And heads for the lake.

1646
Watching from above,
Two egrets stare down into
A garden below.

1647
Climbing up a cliff,
Two worms struggle for position
To win the last race.

1648
Seek on high bare trails,
Sky reflecting violets.
Mountaintop jewels.

1649
The rapids give solace
To the many fish that spawn
Near their shores.

1650
Thistles give me pause.
Do I need to find different
Passage this day?

1651
Undisturbed by sound,
A sleeping bear softly snores,
Giving him away.

1652
Deep in the meadow,
A snake writhes along with a
Snail for company.

1653
Chrysanthemums bloom
While the monk peacefully
Drinks his morning tea.

1654
Dancing mice watch out
For several cats waiting
And looking for you.

1655
The warbler waiting
For a hint from the eagle
That all has gone well.

1656
The accidental
Forest guarded berry plants,
Living borrowed time.

1657
Exhausted, I sought
A country inn, but found
Wisteria in bloom.

1658
Birds flying away
South for the winter's snowstorms.
Waiting there sadly.

1659
A sequestered wren
Squats an egg in its new nest,
Waiting for springtime.

1660
High on a mountain,
Two birds of a feather glide
Together for once.

1661
Who says a seagull
Can't find a mate on the sea?
Never believe that.

1662
A dog howls at night
Alone beside the garden.
Waiting for someone.

1663
A lone meadowlark
Cries in the evening sky
Singing me to sleep.

1664
A standing pine rests
Against a wall of my hut
Hoping for sunlight.

1665
When do lonely frogs
Tire of it all, and bluster
Their stories loudly?

1666
Seaweed lies on shores,
Waiting for seagulls to land
And peck it to death.

1667
A floating brown log
Sinks into the deep waters
Forgetting it's lost.

1668
Within the center
Of all flowers, begins a
Small but fragile bud.

1669
Morning glories stand
Where many have before now,
But these have strong stalks.

1670
Thatched roofs allow rain
To drip into my dinner,
Making my soup grow.

1671
Pupfish jumping up,
Catching an errant insect,
Swallowing its life.

1672
Could a group of doves
Challenge an eagle watching
From a distance so far?

1673
Drunken sailors have
Nothing to say, so they pay
Tribute to themselves.

1674
Seven times twenty
Is the number that begins
A night of terrors.

1675
Fireworks entertain
All those who watch and hear
Them explode above.

1676
The darkness above
Creates a spell of sadness
And leaves me alone.

1677
Frozen to my bones,
I stand up, and wipe myself
From the snow and ice.

1678
The scent of plum blossoms
On the misty mountain path.
A big rising sun.

1679
A pan fish struggles
To free itself from my line
And finally does.

1680
A praying mantis
Stalks his victims slowly, glad
To see it end.

1681

Step lightly downward
From the nearest and highest
Steps of briefest life.

1682

An ant recedes from
A cat's paw, playing deadly
Games of life and death.

1683

Under the same roof,
Courtesans too are asleep.
Bush clover and the moon.

1684

Paradise staggers
Like a drunken grandfather,
Seeking his revenge.

1685

Disappearing sky.
Where do you go when the clouds
Cover your blue light?

1686

Glimmering moonlight,
Brightening the darkest spot
In my hut tonight.

1687

A ticklish problem
Found me alone in my house
Waiting for you.

1688
Wood chopping in the
Distance, dancing sparks and Chips.
Prodigious the maelstrom.

1689
A snake sneaks into
The door to my hut, singing
Songs of warriors lost.

1690
The houses of the
Dead cannot bring back the life
That once belonged here.

1691
Sneaking in the door
From the rear of my bedroom,
A sulking mother.

1692
Calligraphic art
Makes the thing that it depicts
Much better I see.

1693
A sliver of light
Catches my eye as I might
Look at the bright moon.

1694
Eggs in my basket.
Unhappy hens in my yard.
What happens next?

1695
Tiny bugs flying
Around my head in summer.
Where are you winter?

1696
Cancel your mealtime,
The sunset's colors have come,
Making life worthwhile.

1697
The rugs on my floor
Soak up my silt tea like rags,
But save it for me.

1698
Second to no one,
Grandfather greets grandmother
With a simple kiss.

1699
Sometimes things happen
Just because they happen not
Because of reason.

1700
Cruel animals
Treat one another badly
When the weather's bad.

1701
Clouds rain down on us,
Making the day cold and wet.
Why must it be so?

1702
The view from my window
Includes the rice field in snow.
Which rice? Which snow?

1703
Buddha leaves our town,
Making his way up the slopes
Toward the mountain's heights.

1704
Off the deepest end,
A plover takes his chances.
It's now or never!

1705
The clowns never rest,
Making us laugh as the sun
Sets in the west.

1706
Long lost lovers stand
Watching the sunset's glowing
Lights in the night sky.

1707
Along the river banks,
Several frogs lie in the sun,
Ready for nothing.

1708
New clouds quietly form
Above the high mountain peaks,
Gathering moisture.

1709
In the dead of night,
Shadows lie asleep waiting
For a new day.

1710
A spider takes a chance.
Steps slowly over to the
River and swallows.

1711
My mother's uncle
Climbs down from the high tree
Tops and gathers his plums.

1712
As the sky gets dark,
So go the sounds of the day.
Wait for tomorrow.

1713
Alcohol can drown
The best intentions of all
Who swallow it.

1714
Wind dancers fall down
When they don't mind their
Business, and watch down below.

1715
Early morning frost.
From the brothels of Muro
The scent of hot soup.

1716

Lighting one candle
With another candle,
An evening in spring.

1717

Call the robins in
From the apple trees where they
Stand watching the rain.

1718

Whitening gardens
Seem strange from my windowsill.
The snow gently falls.

1719

Standing by the gate,
Several guests gather round
To whisper their thoughts.

1720

Umbrellas make rain
Drip from their edges onto
The garden below.

1721

When rivers come down
From mountains so high above,
They hasten their way.

1722

Calico cats and
Colorful mice together
Make odd couples.

1723
Along the road there goes,
A man with many woes, to
Morn his angry fits.

1724
Mothers and children
Playing with one another.
Why must they ever stop?

1725
Colorful teacups
Balancing in their saucers
Gave me happiness.

1726
On the wharfs of seas,
Fishermen gather to fish,
Telling tall stories.

1727
All day long,
Yet not long enough for the
Skylark, singing, singing.

1728
Tolerance of rains
Give grandfathers the right to
Take naps during them.

1729
Winter storms often
Come in swarms of whirling snow
And give affections.

1730
Moth be gone I say.
Find the fire that beckons you,
And leave me alone.

1731
Who can tell a finch
Which way to wander in life?
For I know not.

1732
My grandfather walks
Slowly toward the meadow now.
Too late for his words.

1733
Peaches in the room
Giving everything a touch
Where wanderers sigh.

1734
Now and then a fly
Flies by my hut and shows its
Green back to my eyes.

1735
Islands in the sun
Drift idly by my chickens
Never giving them thoughts.

1736
Morning glories die,
Forever after in mind.
Never forgetting.

1737
Beggars lying low
Give credence to everything
They sow, and then die.

1738
Stagnant waters still
Measured by their tolerance
Of one day's snowfall.

1739
Floating on the river,
Blossoms from the cherry trees
Disappear from view.

1740
Ravens flying through
The clouds above me into
Bright sunlit days.

1741
So many stars,
Singing their way into me,
Making me hope for more.

1742
The smallest firefly
Makes the biggest light when he
Shows his mate his shine.

1743
Farther above me
Now sits a warbler waiting,
Looking for his mate.

1744
My feet in water.
I hesitate to walk since
The earth will eat me.

1745
Blinding light above,
Searing its brightness onto
The deep snow below.

1746
How does a sparrow
Reach to the top of the sky
And never fall down?

1747
Cast an iron hand
Over all the land and
Never give it up.

1748
Can you imagine
What the old man would do if
The bear yawned out loud?

1749
Singing while raining
Fills up your throat with water.
Not a good prospect.

1750
Spring rain holding an
Umbrella and looking at
The books in a shop.

1751
In the briefest day,
Even the wren calls a break.
Waiting for his lunch.

1752
Tired magpies sitting,
Stretching their wings as wide as
Possible today.

1753
New Year's decoration.
The table with my ink stone
Becomes narrow.

1754
A stick bends and breaks.
But only bows in the wind
The wren hasn't moved.

1755
Twenty-two blackbirds,
Sitting in a row on a
Fence behind my hut.

1756
What does it mean that
Several frogs sing with joy
For no reason?

1757
Fire lives bright tonight
As I sit by the river
And think about death.

1758
Too many robins
Make the sun disappear and
Come not back 'til dawn.

1759
Lightning and thunder
Go together in spirit,
But not in truth.

1760
Everywhere I look,
The soft hills reflect the sun,
Lighting my way.

1761
Stand firmly at last.
For the presence of eagles
Makes all easier.

1762
Traveling by foot,
Protects all the birds and deer
From almost nothing.

1763
Our fountain brings joy
To everyone but my son,
Who never says so.

1764
Wrens sing melodies
That make me dance forever.
Is that such a shame?

1765
Picnics in afternoons
Make the meadows sing with joy
And make me happy, too!

1766
The stream beside me
Grumbles the sounds of deep
Anger and sorrow.

1767
The rice has black seeds,
Where none should be apparent.
What does this mean?

1768
Can I write haiku?
Or must you do it for me?
Said the meadowlark.

1769
Two times two is five.
Or so says the sparrow now
That it is too late.

1770
Can acorns hear me
If I give them a chance to?
Or else am I lost?

1771
I sit in my chair
And wonder about the world
Around me instead.

1772
How can you not care
If the bear does not either
When the skies are dark?

1773
The depths of the sea,
Frighten me into giving
Bells to the chapel.

1774
A line of black trees
Makes the forest intricate,
Without slumbering.

1775
The canyon's flowers
Brighten the old wilderness
Into youth again.

1776
On my wet rooftop,
My cat sits unruffled and
Waiting for breakfast.

1777
Bright lights over the
Mountains give the horizon
Forty-two shadows.

1778
Clothes hanging on lines,
Whipping in the wind about,
And causing mayhem.

1779
Wrens sit on branches,
Seeing what they can see of
The fire in my hut.

1780
Nonsense, said the owl.
How can we ever know this?
And the bear agreed.

1781
Outside of my house,
A nightmare of warring life
Scrambles for survival.

1782
Wherever one goes,
Blackbirds will follow you there,
And peck at your eyes.

1783
No one likes lightning.
Too much of a chance to strike
Anyone standing.

1784
Too few thunderclaps
To confuse us as we go
About our business.

1785
Brandishing a limb,
Grandfather approaches the
Chickadee's bedside.

1786
Somewhere in the sky,
At a different time and place,
The moon did not rise.

1787
Ashen faces look
Upon the desert of my
Night of wandering.

1788
For the first time I
Couldn't believe what I heard,
The stream told the fish.

1789
The silken weaves
Of a spider's deadly web
Make me wonder.

1790
Looking into night
Makes the bright day seem
Brighter as we see the stars.

1791
As a younger boy,
My mother never gave me
Anything to do.

1792
Long ago when the
Cities in the sky were young,
And I could not cry.

1793
Seeing grandfather
Lying in front of the stove
Keeping his feet warm.

1794
Tasting the ice cream,
Makes tongues and mouths cold and
Dead from exhaustion.

1795
Several bluebirds
Travel in pairs flying high
Into the sky above.

1796
Following along,
My old dog came leaping
Into my strong arms.

1797
Can no one hear me?
I cry out so everyone
Can, but no one does.

1798
No one ever dies,
But travels through the meadow
Into the forest.

1799
How can the wood thrush
Capture our hearts through its
Call when no one hears it?

1800
The bumblebees buzz,
Sniffing the flowers around,
And making me sneeze.

1801
Leaves falling from trees,
Hiding the dandelions
From view and from you.

1802
How can a good stew
Not make me happy and new?
My daughter asks me.

1803
In the morning dew
Come armies of mosquitos
Ready for battle.

1804
Gophers digging holes,
Forever dashing hopes for
My garden's success.

1805
Bears and their shadows
Fear not evil, for they have
Future on their side.

1806
A small lizard crawls
Up toward the mountain's highest
Peaks and pinnacles.

1807
Guide me up to thee,
Says the robin as he dies.
To me and you.

1808
Over evening mists
Come herons flying southward
Toward more heated realms.

1809
Covering the rice,
The storm comes boldly forth, and
Tides fall gladly back.

1810
Blades of new bamboo
Knife up through the ground into
Day and night alike.

1811
Ready for shelling,
The snail gets ready to die.
Not another day.

1812
Shelter in the woods
Comes not from sinister men,
But from evil deeds.

1813
Prayer gongs do best
When allowed to ring forever,
Or until they stop.

1814
Thoughts of things to come
Give hawks their sight and ears
And that we cannot know.

1815
Sadder is the tripe
That swims in its sorrows, but
Sadder still, the worm.

1816
Before the whitest
Chrysanthemum, the scissors
Hesitate for a time.

1817
Swans never follow
Strangers when they try to solve
A riddle that they know.

1818
Too many brown ducks
Can fool someone not aware
That ducks dive as well.

1819
Shallow water stops
When knee deep it gets, on legs
That try to swallow me.

1820
Devotion to the Great Saint,
The temple of Ishite,
Rice plants do bloom.

1821

Night and once again,
The while I wait for you cold wind
Turns into rain.

1822

Bridges connecting
Here to there can make it fine
For all to forget.

1823

The desolation of winter
Passing through a small hamlet.
A dog barks.

1824

The wild geese take flight,
Low along the railroad tracks,
In the moonlit night.

1825

Seven words for you,
And seven for me makes two.
Nothing works like that.

1826

Around the bending
River, makes it seem like the
Water likes it, too.

1827

A warbler sneaks west,
When he should go north or south,
Patronizing me.

1828
Barley makes a man
Happy when brewing his beer,
But sad when he stops.

1829
Sowers of the seeds
Need to watch what they step on,
Unless they want mush.

1830
Harvesting the rice
Can be terrifying, too.
If you don't watch out.

1831
A strange thing happened.
A summer's day reformed into
A winter's night.

1832
Too many blossoms,
Drowning in the deep waters.
Catch them if you can.

1833
Don't let the robin
Fly into your soup, for he
Will add nothing there.

1834
Stepping on a rock,
Signaling for the ferry,
Neglected old man.

1835
Several finches
Squabbling among themselves for
Living together.

1836
Boundaries give rise
To makers of lies about
Who doesn't own what.

1837
Truth goes quietly,
While lies go ever loudly
Into the night air.

1838
The nightingale sings
For her lunch and dinner meals.
For breakfast she sleeps.

1839
Scrawny bristle toe,
Never lets a chance go by
For sticking to your leg.

1840
Lanterns on a boat,
Floating by my hut waving.
Trout go dancing by.

1841
Moonflowers give light.
An evening breeze follows me
Down the trail tonight.

1842
Can you tell me why
The snow falls whenever I
Don't want it to?

1843
Early morning frost.
Spider webs with dew on them.
What is on his mind?

1844
The snake gourd blossoms.
My throat blocked with phlegm.
I am already a Buddha.

1845
Sacrificing love,
The lover forsakes all things
For the love of love.

1846
A late summer
Cicada, at the top of his voice,
Chirping and chirping.

1847
The sun sets behind
A traveling monk, tall
In the withered field.

1848
Barren fields of rice,
Indomitable spirits,
A grumbling old man.

1849
Glorious tonight's moon.
Thanks to the darkest clouds
That come to give us rest.

1850
No one should admit,
They cannot tell a liar
From a scarecrow's look.

1851
The swallows greet me
With their cranky shouts and
Calls. The bear sings a song.

1852
Moonlight slanting through
This long bamboo grove
And nightingale songs.

1853
Downwind the rowboat
Dances on the windy lake,
And trusts its driver.

1854
The wintery stream
Boils around rocks and branches
As it heads for death.

1855
Never trust a falcon.
For as much as he tells truth,
He lies for his meals.

1856
My impossible
Blackened peas came crossing my
Daily old routines.

1857
Dying before me,
He asked only one last thing
That I remember.

1858
The evening breezes
Blow softly on the water,
Says the swallow's wife.

1859
White as the snowfall,
Falling on the icy lake's
Waters and drowning.

1860
Waters far away,
Lapping at shores so distant,
I cannot be there.

1861
Bones give me shelter
From my enemies and friends,
The hope in me says.

1862
Stepping on shadows
Makes the hollow man struggle,
And me go to sleep.

1863
Touching the moonlight,
Eating the earth, and braving
The sunlight for you.

1864
Stepping through water
Makes my boots seem heavier,
And my soul lighter.

1865
Never squander love.
You know not what it might
Mean, the owl hoots at night.

1866
Waves of light blue wash
Over the sands near my hut,
And give me their hands.

1867
Music to my ears,
The chickadees signaling
Who should go second.

1868
The butterfly is perfuming
Its wings with the scent
Of the orchid.

1869
Crescent moon does hide,
When the clouds come breezing by,
And cover its light.

1870
That great blue oak,
Indifferent to all blossoms,
Appears nobler.

1871
Cherry blossom pie,
With the price of grain so high,
The butterfly asks.

1872
Spring so very soon!
They are setting the scene for it.
Plum tree and moon.

1873
From this day on,
The inscription in dew on
The bamboo hat be gone.

1874
Into the night, comes the
Sound of the thrushes, woken
By the colors of dawn.

1875
Canceling fireworks
Makes everyone sad tonight.
Especially the moon.

1876
Too many thickets
To favor the one over
The other for rhyme.

1877
Always raking leaves,
While winds tumble them again,
The old man wonders.

1878
Stumbling on branches
Makes the wren angry and sad.
For it now must fly.

1879
How can the tree stump
Sink any further into
The horsefly's nocturne.

1880
Planting rice while
Singing songs can be more
Lovely than anything else.

1881
The bright harvest moon
Keeps me walking all night long,
Around the little pond.

1882
The moon about to appear.
All present tonight with
Their hands on their knees.

1883
White as white can be,
The snowfall does fight with me
For my summer nights.

1884
The moon in the sky
With the sun provide night and
Day at the same time.

1885
Wrapping dumplings in
Bamboo leaves with one finger,
She tidies her hair.

1886
Morning and evening,
Someone waits at Matsushima.
One-sided love.

1887
How wild the sea.
And over Sado Island,
The River of Heaven.

1888
The shadows of crows
Blot out the sun so much that
Even bears do not sleep.

1889
Sleeping on horseback,
The far moon in a continuing
Dream, steam of roasting tea.

1890
An old and deep well
Gave out splashing sounds when
The hail fell from the sky.

1891
A children's rag doll
Lies in the dirt at my feet
And calls out to me.

1892
On the shortcut path,
Stepping through water to cross
In the summer rains.

1893
Thus the gingko leaves
Scatter themselves on the ground,
Where the big bear sleeps.

1894
A pony steps in mud.
A peaceful world interrupts
A street-singer's song.

1895
The loquat blossoms.
Even birds do not like them.
The day is ending.

1896
After the new moon
Gathers its place in the sky,
It then disappears.

1897
Their plum-filled bellies
Endanger their speeds on ground,
Away from the vultures.

1898
Too many green frogs
Can spoil a pond of its fish,
And leave it fallow.

1899
My father's father
Stands alone in the thunder,
Watching me looking.

1900
Candlelight shadows
Move around more than I do,
Making bears restless.

1901
Too many swallows
Make the sky black in their flight,
Confusing the squirrels.

1902
In glowing moonlight,
The whistler makes no sounds,
For the bear must sleep.

1903
Bugs scatter the seeds
From sunset to dawn, while
The gardener sleeps.

1904
Floating in water,
The spider stares at my face,
And wishes for naught.

1905
Warblers sing their songs
While sitting softly on twigs
In forests at night.

1906
The flowers blooming,
Never lasting, colors shining
In the moonlight's glow.

1907
Never trust a bear
Who yawns before he growls,
For he cannot smell.

1908
Eggs before hatching,
Rumble around on the ground,
And the world prepares.

1909
Valley of bamboo,
Where do the rabbits go in
Winter without snow?

1910
Ants climb up the trees
When the rains come falling,
Avoiding the flood.

1911
Hunter before dawn,
Lost all his ammunition,
And left before light.

1912
The peonies bend
In summer's wind across fields
Toward the horizon.

1913
Too many bluebirds
Dazzled my vision with flight,
And puzzled my mind.

1914
No trail to follow
Where the teacher has wandered
Off the end of it.

1915
A boat at anchor
Drifts about the water
Without direction.

1916
Old man's love affair.
In trying to forget it,
A winter rainfall.

1917
Lightning causes me
To close my eyes and see
Its reflection there.

1918
Camphor tree roots
Are quietly getting wet
In winter rainy air.

1919
Evening breeze water
Is slapping against the legs
Of a blue heron.

1920
The autumn morning
Gave no one the feeling that
The day would begin.

1921
Smelling pine gave us
Heavenly scents of lilies
To fend off strangers.

1922
The rain of May time
Facing toward the big river
Homes. Just two of them.

1923
Peony having
Scattered two or three petals
On one another.

1924
The house that burned down
Left behind a sorrowful
Spread of new flowers.

1925
Moon's gathering clouds,
Pushing them out of its way,
With the summer's winds.

1926
My journey has made
Me sick. My dreams wander
The desolate swamps.

1927
Delightful swallows,
Proud of their energies and
Love of the meadows.

1928
A solitary goose
Flies south for a winter's stay.
Trusting no one now.

1929
Apricot blossoms
Loosen their holds on the tree,
And fall to the ground.

1930
In summer brightness,
My eyes catch a hint of a
Blueberry's color.

1931
Slippery white rice
Spills between both my chopsticks
Back onto my plate.

1932
In the twilight hours,
The bells of a temple ring
Into the darkness.

1933
The distant fireworks
Display colors and thunder
In the night's wonders.

1934
Sandals in my hand
Confuses my long journey
From ever ending.

1935
As the lake beckons,
I stand firm and rock solid.
The water's too cold!

1936
Light from a doorway
Lies on the ground to my right
And beckons me forth.

1937
Wolves do not chase me
When I encounter their lair,
For I do not run.

1938
Too many snow days
Brings sadness to everyone,
Morning glories say.

1939
In early summer,
Against a rotting log,
Scattered petals lie.

1940
A wise man never
Trusts a raven with secrets,
An old black bear said.

1941
Cries of a sea hawk
Traveling south for the winter.
The sailor watches.

1942
Guilty consciences
Make for problems when mirrors
Reflect the reasons.

1943
When boats get grounded
After the tides go out to sea,
We never fail.

1944
Novice finches spend
Most of their time entering
Schedules into books.

1945
Waterfalls fall into ponds
That shimmer their warmth into
My heart and my soul.

1946
Mushrooms cancelling
Their season's growth because the
Rains came not this year.

1947
Never fear a muskrat,
For he mumbles and tumbles true
Until night is through.

1948
Light from my candle
Makes shaky shadow puppets
On my walls tonight.

1949
Without turning into
A butterfly, autumn
Deepens for the worm.

1950
Crossing half the sky
On my way toward the mountain,
Big clouds promise snow.

1951
Along my journey
Through this transitory world,
New Year's housecleaning.

1952
A dragonfly trying
To hang on to the upside
Of a blade of grass.

1953
The lightning flashes,
And slashing through the darkness,
A night-heron's screech.

1954
All the more I wish
To see in blossoms at dawn,
The face of God.

1955
The oak tree stands tall
On the hill, even into
Cherry blossom time.

1956
As dewdrops drip,
I wish that I could clean up
This lost world of ours.

1957
In my new clothing,
I feel so different I must
Look like someone else.

1958
Moonlighted mountains,
Scattering in the night, now see
The black clouds broken.

1959
Silence of the kind
That mesmerizes winter,
And makes it easy.

1960
How bright the sun,
As it moves across the sky,
And makes shadows die.

1961
Never gift a man
A horse until he's shown it
To his wife and son.

1962
All poor butterflies
Have troubles with their
Raincoats, ankles, and elbows.

1963
Through signified thought,
He heard all the music,
More than composed it.

1964
Snails have shells around,
And leave a slick reminder
For all to follow.

1965
Cherry blossoms fall
To ground that catches gladly
And scatters them around.

1966
Spring everywhere now,
Even in the bushes with snakes,
And in lakes and ponds.

1967
Nightfall on a lake
Makes fish jump higher, higher
Still in the still air.

1968
Reminder that the
Winter's moon is not colder,
But it is brighter.

1969
Against the windows,
My cat loves to sit and watch
The clouds scamper by.

1970
Water snakes love to
Hide out of sight to ensure
That they won't be found.

1971
To the kitchen door
Come grandchildren no more,
For grandmother's gone.

1972
The chrysanthemums
Give us their wonderful scents
And mosquito nets.

1973
Winter's dark tension
Builds its sunsets into full
Explosive thunders.

1974
Emboldened squirrels
Leave small droppings for us to
Remember them by.

1975
The little foxes.
Emeralds dazzle with bright
Diamonds tonight.

1976
Wandering herons
Fly overhead dropping notes
For my scared rabbits.

1977
For her new wardrobe.
She picks a dress of flowers,
And gives them to me.

1978
Orange apricots,
Hanging from the tree behind,
Will you let me taste?

1979
The bone gatherer.
Where did you come from, and
Where do you go now?

1980
Drinking in the clouds,
My mind wanders towards the
Past, like a magnet might.

1981
Light from my window
Shines on my bed, where I should
Be lying down now.

1982
Still telling lies, the
Old man stands in the mud and
Shouts for someone's help.

1983
The harvest moon shines
Over the meadow at me,
Winking its eye.

1984
From the deep waters,
Comes the sound of the otters,
Clapping their hands.

1985
Eyelids drooping now.
The sun on my face looking
Up to the white clouds.

1986
With beaten down paths
To your noble feats of joy,
Go lightly and soft.

1987
By the water's edge,
My reflection shimmers in
The face looking back.

1988
Summer sun so hot,
Give me a chance to wander
Away from your sight.

1989
The rain lasts so long,
That my ears tire of the sounds
The drops make landing.

1990
Footsteps in the snow,
Reminding me of no one
That I know.

1991
How joyful to cross
Over the river without
Getting my back wet.

1992
After the storm passed,
I waited for the winds to
Disappear as well.

1993
The bridge over the creek
Gives me a suggestion of
Blueberry biscuits.

1994
Above the frosted
Earth, the stars twinkle brightly,
And welcome me home.

1995
The days become slow,
Now that the solstice has passed,
And winter's here.

1996
Loneliness prevails,
Whenever the clouds drift by
Overhead of my house.

1997
Miles and miles of frost,
Whitening the lazy brown grass,
For winter's coming.

1998
White blooming plum tree,
Waiting for a butterfly,
To land on its limbs.

1999
A field of oak trees,
Blowing in the summer breeze,
Gives me happiness.

2000
In the clear water,
A cool trout swims forward and
Back, on his way home.

David Cope has written many non-fiction books and articles on music and artificial intelligence. The machine programs that created a great many of the haiku presented here are described in his upcoming book "The Transcendent Machine." He currently lives in Santa Cruz, California and Santa Fe, New Mexico with his wife of forty-five years Mary Jane Cope. When writing fiction he uses the pseudo-name D. H. Cope to avoid confusion with the poet and novelist David Cope.